70 Years of India's Independence

70 Years of India's Independence

N Vittal, IAS
Dr PK Agrawal, IAS
Sunil K Gulati, IAS
Dr AP Maheshwari, IPS
Dr NC Asthana, IPS
Lt Col Sunil S Parihar
Vivek Garg, Advocate & RTI Activist

Manas Publications
(We Convert Fighters into Writers)
New Delhi - 110 002 (INDIA)

MANAS PUBLICATIONS
(We Convert Fighters into Writers)
(Publishers, Library Suppliers, Importers & Exporters)
4402/5-A, Ansari Road (Opp. HDFC Bank)
Darya Ganj, New Delhi - 110 002 (India)
Phones : Off.: 011-23260783, 23265523, Res.: 011-23842660
E-mail : manaspublications@gmail.com
manaspublications@yahoo.com
Website : www.manaspublications.in

ISBN 978-81-7049-533-8
₹ 995.00

Designed at
Manas Publications

Printed in India at
R.K. Printers, Delhi
and published by Mrs Suman Lata for
Manas Publications, 4402/5-A,
Ansari Road (Opp HDFC Bank),
Darya Ganj, New Delhi - 110002 (INDIA)

Preface

A countrywide, fortnight-long celebration has been planned by the Narendra Modi government to mark 70 years of India's Independence, between August 15 and 22, 2017 along with the celebration of the 75th anniversary of the Quit India movement, to 'rekindle the spirit of patriotism' among citizens.

Minister for Information and Broadcasting M Venkaiah Naidu promises to organise a mega show involving the government and citizens at more than 150 locations. "This is to make the new generation remember the contribution of freedom fighters, especially those who have remained unsung in the past," he said. Around 150 places connected to the freedom movement have been identified and 75 Union Ministers will travel there during this period. "Each Minister will travel to at least two of these places in different States," Venkaiah Naidu said.

Prime Minister Narendra Modi would also participate in these programmes apart from his customary address to the nation. Women ministers had been asked to travel to the border areas and tie rakhi to jawans to include them in the celebrations and emphasise their contribution in protecting the borders.

Freedom fighters and jawans who received gallantry awards would be felicitated. Promotion of khadi and sports meets were some of the events being worked out.

The Human Resource Development (HRD) Ministry would organise essay competitions in schools on the general theme of the struggle for Independence. Patriotic films and songs would be broadcast on Doordarshan and All India Radio. Venkaiah Naidu said, "It is not a party programme. We appeal to all other political parties to take part in the way they would like to and make it a success."

The book highlights the views of top personalities in civil/police/defence set-up of the country's governance who have tackled various kinds of problems, good as well as bad for the people and the country, and offered their opinion to meet the challenges. The views expressed by each contributor are their own and do not necessarily reflect the views of the government. There has been a major shift in Indian politics and governance since 2014. The same has also been briefed in this book.

Vivek Garg

Contents

Contributors

N Vittal, IAS: Former Central Vigilance Commissioner, Government of India. As an IAS (1960 batch, Gujarat Cadre), he spent 42 years in public governance. Worked closely with top leaders in policy making levels both in Gujarat State and in the Government of India and thus have an insider's perspective based on actual experience in the governing philosophy of the Government of India. Eminent writer of many books and articles on governance, political corruption in India.

Dr PK Agrawal, IAS, retired Additional Chief Secretary and Commissioner General, Land Reforms, Government of West Bengal. He worked for eleven years in Land Reform set-up of West Bengal and has long experience in implementation of Land Reforms. He is an eminent writer of sixty books in English and Hindi.

Sunil K Gulati, IAS of 1984 Batch of Haryana cadre is Additional Chief Secretary, Forest and Wildlife, Haryana. He is an IIT Kanpur, IIM Graduate and a Naturopath who has not taken any allopathic medicine for last 22 years. He is an author of 14 books, 2 book chapters and 27 research papers published in India and abroad and has received around 25 Awards in his career so far, including President's Census Medal. Currently he is doing his PhD on Managing and Planning of Long-Term Care of Elderly in India from IIT Delhi.

Dr AP Maheshwari, IPS is ADG (BSF). He belongs to 1984 batch of Uttar Pradesh Cadre. He is a well-known author and has written books on counter insurgency operations and on many other subjects.

Dr NC Asthana, IPS (1986 batch, Kerala Cadre), is a nuclear physicist by training and the celebrated author of as many as 38 critically-acclaimed high-level reference books on various professional subjects and some 80 research papers. He has extensive experience of intelligence and counterinsurgency operations in all the three major trouble spots of the country: Kashmir, left-wing extremism and the North-East.

Lt Col Sunil S Parihar: Masters in Psychology, after taking early retirement he continues to keep abreast with military matters.

Vivek Garg: Advocate and RTI Activist and writer on current topics.

1

India at 70: An Inspiring Saga of Resilience

N Vittal

India is now entering its 70th year of independence from the British rule on 15th August 1947. I belong to that generation which was the last under the colonial rule and chronologically, the first in post-independent India. This gives me a unique place in time to record my perceptions as an Indian who loves his motherland.

I was born on 31st January 1938 just about a decade before India became independent. I still cherish vivid memories of my excitement and joy of celebrating India's independence as a student of 6th standard in Bishop Heber High School, Puthur Tiruchirapalli in Tamil Nadu. I still recall how all of us students marched on the streets singing the patriotic inspiring songs of the great Tamil poet Subramania Bharati, which were banned in the British times! The poet himself had to seek refuge in the French-held Pondicherry for a decade in his life!

Reaching the age of 79 shortly, I feel greatly inspired. In fact, if we take a holistic view of our existence as a nation, all of us can be very proud of our motherland, India that is Bharat and rejoice in the fact that as an independent nation, in the last 70 years, our country has blazed an inspiring saga of resilience.

This has many dimensions to this achievement. As I see it, we can examine this saga of resilience from the following angles:

(i) The welding of our country as a single nation.

(ii) Our exciting exercise of emerging as the world's largest functioning democracy.

(iii) Demonstrating resilience in facing and overcoming both man-made and natural challenges in the last seven decades.

(iv) Discovery and rediscovery of our cultural roots and values which make us unique in the comity of nations.

WELDING OF INDIA AS A NATION

We can begin with the welding of our nation. In fact, when India became independent, there were a lot pessimistic voices and fears expressed by many like Winston Churchill about the future of our country. There were those who said that India was a geographic expression, and not a nation in the modern twentieth century sense. What we inherited from the British was a country of subcontinental dimensions, two-thirds of which was directly under the British rule and another one-third with the nearly 600 native States which covered wide spectrum from large States like Baroda, Mysore, Indore, Patiala, Hyderabad to petty principalities, 200 about them in the Saurashtra peninsula alone in Gujarat. In addition, there were vast regions in the North-East and North-West where the tribals were more or less independent having their own traditional forms of governance. These mountain tribes like the Nagas had a very tenuous relationship with the British as the paramount power.

We were fortunate to have a unique leader in Sardar Vallabhbhai Patel who within a year and half was able to weld the whole conglomeration of States into one nation. The only outstanding problem which he was not allowed to be tackled was Jammu and Kashmir thanks to the intervention of Jawaharlal Nehru which still continues to haunt us.

Sardar Patel also had the vision to realize that the country has to govern itself and the excellent Civil Service (the steel frame of India built by the British) which had 411 members of Indian Civil Service should be retained as a core, built the administrative framework for the governance of the country. These two significant contributions of Sardar Patel will ever be enshrined in the history of modern India as unparalleled contributions for laying the foundation for India as a modern nation.

The last 70 years since independence has witnessed a lot of turbulence and there have been continuous interlay between regional forces and the national forces. The linguistic reorganization of the States in 1956 gave a boost to the growth of regional languages and regional forces and even today the tension between the forces for irredentism and regional assertion continue to haunt different part of the country. Even after seventy years, regional forces seem to thrive. Sometimes these may come in the way of national progress.

Irredentism according to *The Concise Oxford Dictionary* is a term that originated in the context of the 19th century Italian politics. It was used to describe the demand for the restoration of the territories lost by it.

According to an article by Swapan Dasgupta in *The Times of India*, Chennai edition, 4th September 2016, in the Indian context, this term was liberally bandied about pejoratively to describe the RSS demand for Akhand Bharat. Dasgupta goes on to focus in the article on the decision taken by the Mamata Banerjee government in West Bengal to substitute the name of the State with Bangla/Bengal/Bangal.

Dasgupta traces in his insightful article the emotional attachment of the Bengalis to their language and the shared memories of an united Bengal. He traces the significance of the first partition of Bengal in 1905 initiated by Viceroy Lord Curzon and the tragic partition of Bengal for the second time when India became independent in 1947. He ends the article by saying "even as India and Bangladesh move towards a stable relationship, the delusions of the past have finally been junked. Irredentism has been issued a death certificate decades after its actual death."

It is interesting that when we look at our history the interplay between irredentism and regionalism seems to have been an under-appreciated recurring theme. At least three parallel cases come readily to my mind.

The first and perhaps the oldest, is the Dravidian movement in Tamil Nadu which can be traced back to 1910 with the formation of the Justice Party. This party consisting of well to do leaders of the south Indian community who were not Brahmins. They and their party were focused on ensuring that the dominance of the Brahmins in Tamil Nadu under the British government, thanks to their taking up early to English education and their command over the English language, should be challenged. They succeeded in their effort and as the freedom movement gathered momentum, in the first three decades of the twentieth century, captured political power under the reform legislations successively enacted by the British to encourage local self-government.

By a curious twist of history, it was again the Brahmins who dominated the Congress Party which led the freedom movement and the Justice Party found itself supporting the British government in the '20s and '30s. The advent of Gandhiji brought a dramatic change in widening the appeal of the Congress and making it an umbrella party for the freedom struggle.

In 1946 the Justice Party had lost its momentum and was reborn as the Dravida Kazhagam (DK) under the leadership of redoubtable Erode V Ramasamy Naicker popularly known as Periyar. Ironically, he was a close associate of Rajaji and an active leader of the Congress Party, who had radical ideas on social reform. He was a Kannadiga hailing from Erode and visualized Dravida Nadu as inclusive of all the southern States of Tamil Nadu, Andhra Pradesh, Telangana, Karnataka and Kerala. One strong element behind the Dravida concept was the unique and historic position of Tamil as an ancient classical language and linguistically the mother of Kannada, Malayalam and Telugu. The Dravidian movement not only emphasized the separate identity of the southern States and moved for social reform, abolition of differences between castes and social equality. Most importantly, it did not accept the concept of a united India. In short, the behaviour of the Tamils in the Dravidian movement was similar to the irredentists in the

Italian movement led by Garibaldi and Mazzini in the 19th century.

Unfortunately, the rest of the southern States like Andhra, Kerala and Karnataka did not buy this idea championed by the Dravida Kazhagam and its offspring the Dravida Munnetra Kazhagam (DMK).

In fact, they claimed their own languages to be also ancient classical languages. Soon after the Atal Bihari Vajpayee government conferred the status of classical language on Tamil, in the year 2000, all the three also ended up getting a similar status! This has been upheld recently by the Madras High Court. In short, regionalism had triumphed over irredentism.

A further reiteration of this trend is what happened in 2013 when Telangana was separated from Andhra Pradesh. It must be recalled that soon after independence in 1947, it was the strong demand for Vishal Andhra as a State based on the Telugu language and the enormous emotional movement resulting in the fast unto death of Potti Sreeramulu in 1952 that compelled Jawaharlal Nehru to concede to the demand and form Vishal Andhra including the regions of Madras presidency in British India, Telangana and Rayalaseema. The formation of Andhra gave a further boost to the linguistic re-organization of States which took place in 1956.

A third example of the triumph of regionalism is in Maharashtra. The separation of Gujarat and Maharashtra in 1960 as a result of the Samyukta Maharashtra and the Maha Gujarat movements following the 1956 linguistic re-organization of States did not put an end to the growth of regionalism.

The formation of Shiv Sena in 1966 based mainly on job opportunities for Mumbaikars showed that regionalism can flourish on the basis of not only language but on economic factors.

Maharashtra has a remarkable place in Indian history. The coming together of the Maharashtrians under the inspired leadership of Chhatrapati Shivaji, who in turn was inspired by the vision of Samarth Ramdas, was a golden period in our history. The Maharashtrian confederacy in the 17th and 18th century dominated practically the whole of the country providing challenges to the authority of the Mughal empire and the emerging colonial powers of the British, French and the Portuguese.

The Shiv Sena by appealing to the Marathi Manus is similar to the irredentists of the Italian movement. Nevertheless today the demand for Vidarbha which is raised from time to time shows that the dynamics of irredentism versus regionalism is not a closed chapter in our country.

As has happened in Tamil Nadu, Andhra Pradesh and now Bengal, will Maharashtra also see regionalism triumph?

DEMOCRACY AND GOOD GOVERNANCE

This growth of regionalism has had its impact on politics also and continues to haunt the politics of today and perhaps in foreseeable future. That brings us to the second angle of politics and governance in the country. The most significant achievement in the 70 years of our existence as a modern nation is our becoming an open, vigorous, live democracy. The magnitude of achievement of India on this aspect can be realized only when we see, how many of the countries which became independent after the Second World War were able to retain their democratic structure in essence and many of them we find became victims of dictatorship or military rule. This achievement is due to the number of factors and perhaps and basically it relates to the long tradition of self-government and the concept of Dharma or the right conduct is more important than the power of the ruler which is unique in our culture. The most serious challenge to democracy after independence arose when Prime Minister Indira Gandhi imposed emergency for a period of 2 years from 25th June 1975 to January 1977. It is a fact that she ultimately displayed the spirit and commitment to the need for legitimacy as a democratically elected leader is the one which made her call for election in which she was roundly defeated.

The fact that the very same Indira Gandhi came to power in 1980 is again a demonstration about the genuineness of the preparation and operational democracy in our country and the fact that the people have imbibed the essence of democracy and the values of democracy which ultimately is the best form of governance.

As Churchill pointed out, there are people who consider democracy as the worst form of governance. We all realise that the other forms of governance are much worse. The Constitution of India which we adopted in January 1950 has served our nation well and the three pillars of governance visualized in our Constitution namely, the Legislators for enacting the laws, Judiciary for interpreting the laws and the Executive for implementing the laws, both political as well as permanent civil services have served the country well. What is significant is the role played by other important institutions of democracy. A free press and the media is vital for democratic functioning and Indian media for the last 70 years has been by and large free. There have been only limited period when censorship had been imposed as during the period of emergency. Judiciary has by and large maintained independence except in some rare instances where it laid down the standard, judiciary coming up with the concept like the basic structure of the Constitution has proved very essential to ensure that functioning of the democracy is not subject to the whims and fancies of the political pressures of the day.

Perhaps, more important and increasingly more realized is the role played by certain specific institutions, two of which needs special mention, namely, the Election Commission of India and the Comptroller and Auditor General of India. These two institutions which are mentioned in the Constitution have been headed by eminently competent and fair minded and effective public servants who have made these institutions models for emulation by others.

Particular mention must be made of a remarkable Chief Election Commissioner TN Seshan who demonstrated how powers of conducting free and fair elections conferred on the Election Commission of India can be exercised effectively to counter the money power and muscle power as well as wide check corruption in electoral processes. It is true that we have not yet succeeded fully. There has been a significant progress in this direction.

One might ask, not got still the perfect system, but we can justifiably claim that say of all the electoral systems and institutions conducting elections in democracies in the world, our system perhaps is among the best, if not the best.

This was dramatically displayed to the world at the time of the 2000 US Presidential elections. In that election when the counting of the votes between the two candidates Al Gore and George W Bush became a long drawn conundrum ultimately to be resolved by the Supreme Court of the United States.

The use of the electronic voting machines and imaginatively brilliant concept of independent machines which effectively safeguards the machines from electronic bugs and viruses perhaps is not appreciated still in our country to the extent needed.

It is true that after all these years we may still have a lot of problems about the functioning of these different institutions and at present the judiciary has been complaining about the difficulties they face about shortage of Judges and lack of infrastructure and resources and general complaint about the judiciary is about the delays in the system. But the very fact that there is ecology where different wings of the governance are in touch with each other and there is healthy exchange of views and accommodation is a reassurance that our nation will remain resilient so far as developing effective democracy and preserving our system are concerned.

MEETING CHALLENGES OF MAN-MADE AND NATURAL DISASTERS

That brings us to perhaps one of the most cheerful, happy aspects of the resilience of our nation. This is the saga of how individuals, inspired leaders and organizations rose to the occasion to meet the challenges on a wide range of fronts. These challenges were both natural as well as man made. Let us begin with the natural challenges.

The first natural challenge was the problem of feeding such a large country. In the last days of the British Rule in 1943, the Great Bengal Famine demonstrated how devastating could be the impact of famine, if there was poor governance. Economists like Amartya Sen have demonstrated, it is not so much the availability of water and resources that matter, as the quality of governance and the capacity of the people to buy food to save themselves. The Green Revolution, it was about under the inspired efforts of C Subramaniam as a Minister-in-charge of Agriculture; B Sivaraman (ICS), Secretary, Agriculture; Dr MS Swaminathan as the expert in Agriculture is a saga that is required to be cherished in gold in the history of our country. From being a pathetic position of depending from a ship to mouth situation, these leaders and the government of India rose to the occasion to bring out the Green Revolution.

Equally remarkable has been the White Revolution spearhead by Dr Verghese Kurien, based in Anand (Gujarat), was able to make the Amul Milk Union Limited and later on through 'Operation Flood' see to it that India became largest producer of milk in the world and the milk products. The White Revolution was no less than the Green Revolution and it had a lot of multiplier benefits in terms of empowering of women and the rural population. The third had been the Blue Revolution relating to the nuclear power.

Homi Bhabha and Satish Dhawan, are the names which are remembered by grateful nation who led the revolution in both atomic energy and space technology. When sceptical scientists in the West questioned Bhabha how India could manage to have nuclear scientists and engineers for harnessing the nuclear power? Bhabha supposed to have said, "remember that for we have a tradition going back to 5,000 years. Our forefathers have been sitting on their bottom and contemplating the infinite. They developed enormous capacity for abstract thinking and blue sky research." This enormous heritage of ours for developing, abstract concepts like mathematics including the concept of zero are the ones which will help us in meeting the challenges of the Blue Sky research which underlies nuclear power as history has shown Bhabha's words proved to be prophetic.

The saga in nuclear power has been repeated even more dramatically in space. India is one of the half a dozen space powers in the world today. The digital age in which we are living and the age of modern communication would not be possible without mastery of the space technology which is the basic infrastructure needed.

The challenges from the scientific front had been met and perhaps even more greater where the challenges of man-made disasters. Many parts of the country are subjected practically for natural calamities like floods, earthquake and even tsunami and much maligned bureaucracy which is accused of red-tape always raises to the occasion and tackle the problems.

During the Bangladesh crisis Indira Gandhi showed her managerial skill that India can tackle the enormous problem of more than a crore refugees.

Government's efforts on such occasions were also supplemented by highly credible and effective NGOs like the Ramakrishna Mission, the RSS and the CSR (Corporate Social Responsibility) initiatives of reputed Indian industrial houses like the Tatas, Mahendras, TVS Group, Godrej and so on.

MATURING OF POLITICAL IDEOLOGIES: THE LEFT AND THE RIGHT

Right from the date of independence, thanks to the enormous clout of Jawaharlal Nehru and the Congress, India was governed by the leftist ideology. Narendra Modi in the 2014 election wrought a miracle. Indian politics shifted tectonically to the right. As India celebrates seventy years of Independence we are witnessing the maturing of the political ideologies, both on the left and on the right.

Ever since the Modi government took office in May 2014, the establishment intelligentsia which has had free and unchallenged run for seventy years, practically the entire spectrum of political, academic and social institutions has been in a state of shock. They are in a mood of denial and practically every action of the Modi government is being viewed with a hostile microscope. In the process, some of the major policy directions and the ideological evolution which the BJP and its basic inspiration, the RSS are undergoing are lost sight of.

One example of the establishment intelligentsia's secular perception about the Modi government and especially, the RSS in an article by G Sampath in *The Hindu* dated 16th February 2016 in connection with the current debate about nationalism arising out of the turmoil in the universities like JNU, Central University at Hyderabad and earlier in IIT (Madras). Sampath in the course of his article makes the following comments:

> "Already, according to the nationalist taxonomy of the Sangh Parivar, Adivasis in central India, Dalit students, Left intellectuals, human right activists, a certain religious

minority, anti-nuclear activists, beef eaters, non-haters of Pakistan, inter-religious couples, homosexuals, and labour activists are anti-nationals. If we take into account Monday's episode of goonda nationalism at Patiala House in New Delhi, we must expand the list to include journalists, people dressed like JNU students, anyone without an identity card, anyone recording goonda nationalists in action, and anyone opposed to the said goonda nationalists.

"At this rate, it seems likely that by the time the National Democratic Alliance (NDA) finishes its term, the vast majority of Indians – who are unfortunately still not members of the Sangh Parivar – would have turned into anti-nationals. The only cure for their anti-nationalism being the healing nationalist brutality of an Akhil Bharatiya Vidyarthi Parishad (ABVP) or Bajrang Dal lynch mob, while India's nationalist police presides over the ceremony, peacefully.

"What exactly is goonda nationalism? A goonda nationalist is anyone who arrogates to himself the job of certifying citizens as anti-national."

He goes on to elaborate,

"Goonda nationalism is not a new phenomenon. The German historian Arthur Rosenberg, in his book *Fascism as a Mass Movement*, refers to two conditions (among others) as prefiguring the rise of fascism: the rise of right-wing nationalism, and an active connivance between the state and identitarian storm troopers. What India has witnessed over the past month, first in Hyderabad Central University

(HCU) and now in JNU, is early consolidation of these two conditions for the furtherance of an agenda that we shall not call fascist because, as we've been assured repeatedly by eminent Indian liberals, India is too diverse and Indian democracy too resilient for us to use the f-word."

"India's bane has been the failure of its self-proclaimed 'constitutional' liberals to acknowledge that the forces of Hindutva and economic liberalism (or neo-liberalism) are a package deal."

"In their heated embrace of economic liberalism, India's liberal elites looked away as the state either went after or neglected the interests of labourers, the urban poor, the farmers, the landless, the land-poor – the vast majority of whom are from socially marginalised castes. Now they find the state looking away as their own liberal freedoms come under siege by state-endorsed illiberal forces."

I am afraid I cannot agree. Has RSS remained frozen in time and is totally unaware or insensitive to the drastic changes that have taken place in the last 80 years since it was founded?

Organizing Shakhas where the members of the Sangh wear khaki shorts and carry out exercises may be reminiscent of the Hitler youth. But the RSS has not remained frozen in time or ideology.

It is surprising that the secular and establishment intelligentsia who consider themselves to be modern and progressive in their thinking and are aware of the developments in the world, somehow assume that organizations other than theirs will remain frozen in time and may not change at all.

An intimate insider's glimpse of what has been happening in RSS itself can be had from a very perceptive book titled *Lost Years of the RSS* by Sanjiv Kelkar published in 2009. Kelkar who has been closely associated with the movement and he gives an insider's perception of the various currents of thoughts and leadership styles of the different Sarsanghachalaks who have led the RSS in the last eighty years.

The initial idea of Dr Hedgewar who founded the RSS on Vijayadashami day in 1925 was only to unite the Hindu community to which majority of the people for our country belongs. But the subsequent development of the RSS under his successor Guruji Golwalkar brought a different approach. Balasaheb Deoras brought further changes.

Nevertheless, there has been a consistent stream of thought through the RSS and reflected in its track record. The basic inspiration comes from Swami Vivekananda and the consciousness/realization that majority of us in this country are inheritors of the Sanatana Dharma which is popularly called Hinduism.

In fact the word Hindu itself is the name given to our religion by the foreigners who could not appreciate the nuances and special aspects of our religion.

As mentioned earlier, the immediate inspiration for the RSS came from Swami Vivekananda. Swami Vivekananda himself was the product of late 19th century social political and religious renaissance especially in Bengal of the Indian and Hindu national consciousness thanks to the impact of the British rule.

There have been two streams of spiritual tradition in our country. One has been the true spiritual quest at the individual level represented by seers like Ramakrishna Paramahamsa, Aurobindo and Ramana Maharshi. The other are reformers who came on scene from time to time and tried to bring about changes in the way of life of Hindus by emphasizing the basic values which constitute the essence of Sanatana Dharma. It is the combined efforts of these two streams that kept our tradition of Hinduism going and this country united as a unique example of unity in diversity, a multi lingual multi-ethnic multi-cultural wonder. When the RSS started, it was inspired by this tradition.

Although the focus of the RSS to begin with was only on holding back to the basic values and culture of the country, as an organization, it could not be indifferent to other aspects of life like politics and governance. That is why the shaping of the organization also was inspired by the parallel development in other fields.

In his book, Kelkar points out how, while the RSS was initially focused only on the concept of Swadeshi, it could not be indifferent to the major international developments like the globalization of the economy and the modern world which is borderless but which is united on the basis of competition and at the same time with the emphasis on ethics in business.

Surprisingly, the collapse of ideologies like Communism has once again created an opportunity for refocusing on the need for ethical element in business. And, it is here that the RSS and BJP with their focus on our cultural roots in Sanatana Dharma have an advantage and a long term inherent robustness over all others opposed to it to deliver good governance of the country.

The Modi government represents the first totally and authentic home grown ideology for ethical or Dharmik good governance operating on the inclusive principle of *sarve jana sukhino bhavantu*.

The voters of India have decisively rejected the left of centre 'secular ideology' that was followed by all post-independent governments since 1947. They have given an opportunity for a genuine Right of centre government.

What we are witnessing is the re-inventing and reshaping of the organizations of both RSS and BJP in the light of the basic principles of Sanatana Dharma. Narendra Modi heading the government and Mohan Bhagwat heading the RSS have found a common frequency of articulating an ideology of the Right of the centre government, tailor-made for our own Indian requirement. They are also laying a firm foundation by harking back to the fundamentals of Sanatana Dharma which have a very close resonance for good governance.

The vision of *'vasudhaiva kutumbakam'* is an inclusive one. So is the Upanishadic dictum of *'Sarve Jana Sukhino Bhavantu, Sarve Pashyantu Bhadrani, Sarve Santu Niramaya'*.

It is this important shift that is taking place which is missed by the current commentators who form the vast majority of the boisterous establishment and 'secular' intelligentsia today.

That is why G Sampath is wrong when he says, "India's bane has been the failure of its self-proclaimed liberals to acknowledge that the forces of Hindutva and economic liberalism (or neo-liberalism) are a package deal."

For seventy years since independence governing philosophy of the government of India, largely influenced by Jawaharlal

Nehru and the leaders of the freedom struggle was distinctly to the left of the centre and totally disconnected from the values of Sanatana Dharma. This development ignored the basic fact that a long term view of India's evolution and the inspiration for such governance, was denied from the eternal teachings of Sanatana Dharma. This spiritual form was universally known as *Bharatvarsha* and *Bharatkhanda*, thanks to a number of tenable factors. The focus on left of centre and complete detachment from the basic roots of national consciousness of us as the children of *Bharatvarsha* was in a sense an artificial temporary aberration. A badly needed corrective has now been provided thanks to the enormous initiative and the drive and as well as the leadership shown by Narendra Modi and the results of 2014 elections. The question is whether as the establishment intelligentsia of today bred over the last seventy years with government patronage will succeed in halting this well needed corrective. In my judgement, Narendra Modi has started on the right lines both on the policy and programme implementation. He rightly emphasised during the election campaign not so much on the religious aspect or Hindutva, but on the needs of good governance. At the same time, he also continuously highlighted the need for cleanliness in public life. The disconnect with the ethical dimension was the great weakness of left of centre governance. The UPA-II government which recorded a history of scandals provided the perfect foil for Narendra Modi to project his alternative vision. This combined with the appeal to the roots of Indian culture and Indian consciousness apparently led to the tectonic shift to the political right. In the articles I wrote in the *Bureaucracy Today*, I have tried to point out how many of the ideas of Narendra Modi are not only in tune with the basic philosophy of the

Sanatana Dharma but also at the same time are eminently pragmatic and doable. Even *Namami Gange* project which prima facie may appear to be a lost cause can be realised in our life time. This in spite of the fact that more than 30 years, ₹30,000 crore have been spent by different governments on this project.

This is because for this government and Modi, Ganga is not merely a river; it is something sacred and innately connected with our Bharatiya consciousness. Anyone who has read Jawaharlal Nehru's *Discovery of India* will realise that even for a thoroughly westernised intellectual like Jawaharlal Nehru, Ganga had its unique appeal. Perhaps, subliminally, Jawaharlal Nehru as one of the great sons of *Bharatvarsha* realised the significance of Ganga representing the cultural essence of this country. As mentioned earlier, the articles which I wrote in the *BT* have been classified for the sake of convenience and coherence into four categories. The first relates to articulating the essential spirit and soul of what constitutes India's political Right and its close association with patriotism and national pride. The realisation that mother country is dearer than heaven. *Janani janma bhumisya sokathathesya hegarishtati*, means that as children of Bharat Mata, we should be alert all the time for our national service and defence. The new approach to defence articulated by the current government perfectly in tune with this significance of the core of India's political right. The other two parts deal with more pragmatic issues of governance. Bulk of these articles relate to governance. Our constitution says that India is a union of States and not a Federation. The criticism of the Narendra Modi government is against Federalism is not correct. Articles on cooperative federalism show that this concept need not be a mere catch word, but can be a pragmatic policy of finding a new meaning in the working of the Constitution. Both, the Government of India and the States, can make their own contribution in building up a 21st century India which will be an economic super power.

If for a moment we shift our focus and take a longer view of history, we find that there are all in these period of long history of more than ten thousand years we find that whenever the Sanatana Dharma was forgotten and our society deteriorated because it moved away from the principle of Sanatana Dharma, it always found its way back to the main core of its cultural soul, thanks to the timely appearance of the right spiritual leaders as well as political leaders. The founding of our Vijayanagara empire in the 14th century and the case of Samarth Ramdas and Shivaji together in the 17th century immediately come to mind. The same could be considered in the past when there have been great leaders of Vaishnava and Shaiva *sampradaya* who have guided the kings and influenced the course of governance for the country.

Even in his famous book *The Continent of Circe: Essays on the People of India*, Nirad Chaudhuri, a self-confessed anglophile, identified this unique characteristic of our country which like a snake shreds its old skin from time to time and always remould itself, thus coming back to its basic values and culture and its concept of Sanatana Dharma again and again.

In a perceptive article in *The Hindu*, dated 5th February 2016, Suhas Palshikar who teaches political science at the Savitribai Phule Pune University, Pune had analysed the evolution of the governance philosophy of BJP. The article titled "Modi-Shah Template for the BJP" published in *The Hindu*, dated 4th February 2016, makes the following interesting comments:

> "In the 10 years after the Godhra riots, Narendra Modi evolved a new model of Hindutva politics. The basis of this model lay in ruthless use of the State apparatus to signal to the minorities where they belonged. Once that was achieved, it was only one step to Hindutva penetrating Gujarati civil society and the popular imagination. Then his focus shifted to improving the macroeconomic performance of the State. The fourth dimension of that model was to focus on the lower middle classes instead of the lower bottom (which was the focus of Dr Manmohan Singh government at the Centre). The 'Gujarat Model' was further augmented by the adoption of an unprecedented and most astute media blitzkrieg. A new BJP was thus born – through the 2007 and 2012 State elections in Gujarat. It travelled to Delhi with Mr. Modi from the time of his speech at Delhi's Shri Ram College of Commerce in early 2013.
>
> "... most fundamentally, for the BJP, which prides in its links with the Rashtriya Swayamsevak Sangh and its espousal of Hindutva, the biggest challenge would be negotiating with its Hindutva ideology. For the past two years, the party is hiding behind the so-called fringe elements. The game plan seems to be that while the 'fringe' functions as storm trooper, the party would slowly make Hindutva politically acceptable. It has neither officially moved away from Hindutva nor formally made efforts to position itself as a part of Hindutva."

In fact, if we take the Sanatana Dharma as the core philosophy of India's political right as represented by BJP today, then the following points become obvious:

> For a long time RSS has been perceived to be a militant form of Hinduism. Veer Savarkar articulated the concept of Hindutva and the secular intelligentsia had always branded RSS as a fascist organisations adopting Hitler's technique depending of violence. Although, some may describe the very aggressive initiative taken by the RSS as the fringe element, the suspicion has always been articulated as a hidden agenda of the BJP. Even when Atal Bihari Vajpayee was at the helm, he was described by Govindachari as a *mukhota*. It was said by 'secular' leaders that Atalji was a right leader in a wrong party and so on. On the other hand, when Narendra Modi reached the helm of affairs, the time had become right for openly accepting the enlightened form of Sanatana Dharma, which invariably has been insisted by all great leaders of Hinduism as the essence of Hinduism can be openly articulated as the governing philosophy or ideology of India's political right. Practically all the great spiritual leaders in ancient and recent times have by their behaviour and action shown that Sanatana Dharma is the essence of Hinduism ultimately means that does not need any militant defence. The great Paramacharya of Shri Kanchi Kamakoti Peetham in the 20th century faced the full onslaught of the anti-Brahmin and atheistic movement lead by vociferous leaders like EV Ramasamy Naicker and the Dravida Kazhagam and the Dravida Munnetra Kazhagam. Over the years, Sanatana Dharma in Tamil Nadu has re-established itself and it is

the atheist movement which seems to have lost steam in the last 70 years.

Nevertheless, it was a fact that there have been in Hinduism itself when the clashes between the different schools of thoughts became violent. There are many examples of militant Hinduism in the past. There were sects like Veerashaivas and Veeravaishnavas. When faced with hostile rule, like that of the Moghuls, Sikhism became the militant defence of Hinduism and there have been other similar movements. But, ultimately, what has remained as a core of Hinduism which has maximum number of followers is the middle of the road of Sanatana Dharma. The RSS drawing inspiration from Vivekananda can easily adopt the significance and long term blessings of Sanatana Dharma and can continue to survive the organisational support and the role of a mentor for the BJP which is more directly concerned with the political governance of the country.

Finally, a simple point which many may overlook, when it comes to the context of invoking the cultural and spiritual dimension of Sanatana Dharma as the unifying and underlying philosophy for the India's political right. The continuous drum beating about the separation of the church and the State and the secular socialistic ideology has perhaps made many Indian themselves inheritors of the rich traditions and spiritual heritage of Sanatana Dharma about how Sanatana Dharma and Hinduism are different from other religions. In 21st century, a nation based only on religion will be called a theocratic State. In fact, the partition of India in 1947 and the Hindu-Muslim violence that preceded it was based on the so called two-nation theory. The liberation of Bangladesh demonstrated once and overall the whole world the fact that religion alone cannot be the binding force for unifying and articulating the identity of a nation. That is where, Sanatana Dharma or Hinduism scores over other religions which do not have its internal vibrancy and time tested intellectual coherence which is a result of more than 5,000 to 7,000 years of history.

As we have seen the Sanatana Dharma inspired and sustained development of skills and also welded with the concept of Dharma helps to really achieve every person professional excellence in every area of human endeavour. That is why, the political right of centre ideology in India, based on Sanatana Dharma will be able to contribute and inspire the whole nation much better than any of the later day philosophies of pure economic or self-interest based ideologies. In other words, Sanatana Dharma can be the basis of a modern forward looking true democratic Republic.

2

Can India Disintegrate? Analysis of Possible Scenarios and How to Avert Them?

Dr NC Asthana

INTRODUCTION

A constant refrain at all forums in the country is the need to preserve the 'unity and integrity' of the country. Don't we wonder why it is so? Why is it that even 70 years after independence we are obliged to make fervent, emotionally charged appeals to our own citizens to preserve the unity and integrity of the country? Do other nations do that? Following the dissolution of the British Empire after the Second World War, as many as 48 countries gained independence in due course. Nowhere do we find such desperation to somehow preserve the unity and integrity of the country. Clearly, something is fundamentally wrong with us.

Note: Views expressed in this article by Dr NC Asthana are personal.

WHAT REALLY AILS US AS A NATION?

In human history, the concept of nations, in the sense of its meaning in modern European political theory, is a relatively recent thing. On the other hand, the people who constitute a nation are a much older thing. The problem of modern realpolitik is to somehow reconcile these two. Whoever people, whichever nation are not able to reconcile these two adequately, are destined to suffer.

India, throughout the course of history, has been essentially a socio-religio-cultural construct of people of diverse races bound by fate to have been born in the same geographical entity with no cohesive force to hold them together and make them work synergistically. It was only the genius Kautilya who first identified this fundamental weakness and tried to enforce the semblance of nationalism back in an era when Europe was far from even thinking on that line. However, because it was the effort of a man far ahead of his times, it lasted only as long as the imperial sceptre was wielded strongly, ruthlessly and intelligently enough. Kautilya too, his genius notwithstanding, did not consider it necessary to enlist the willing support of the people for the '*rashtra*' or nation.

The *conditio sine qua non* for the creation and sustenance of a nation is the consensus among the people constituting it, that they share certain ties without any compulsion whatsoever. The origin of many of the fissiparous tendencies in the body politic of this country may be traced to its unique socio-political legacy and history. The average person residing in the Indian subcontinent was (and still is) characterized so acutely by an obsession with his own self-interests that his parochial loyalties have always been stronger than any other loyalties. Thus, in spite of several common traditions, history, sufferings and glories, one's immediate surroundings were more important for him than what was encompassed within the geographical boundaries of the nation. The considerations of race often took a backseat because the considerations of the subdivisions like caste were paramount. A commonality of economic interests could also never inspire the people, as an essentially fatalistic approach to life had always relegated finance to an unpraiseworthy position. The *tout ensemble* was, therefore, to create a self-centric view of life in which the modern concepts of nation and nationalism *per se* did not even exist. A history of sufferings and subjection could perhaps have made some other people more cohesive – in our case they sowed the seeds of such demoralization that it only made them more reclusive.

People of this land have had one important difference with respect to people of other lands. It is not that only the people of this land have been self-centric and materialistic; others have also been prone to it. However, over the centuries the others learnt to place something else above their parochial and selfish considerations. Thus in spite of all the globalizing premises of modernity, and the inexorable divisive forces generated by the social, economic and political structures, they have evolved a mutually acceptable and paramount consideration of a common nationality which eventually accounts for the stability of the State. We, the people of this land, missed this vital turning point in history, and hence our problems.

Thus the present problems of this land are not really new – they are only modern manifestations of some very old maladies – some more vociferous and violent expressions of

age-old aspirations. Insurgent situations in the Indian context are essentially virulent forms of the identity crises of various small groups. Insurgencies arise whenever some constituents of a nation start developing incongruities with respect to the factors that are supposed to build a nation and hold it together, such as race or ethnicity, religion, language, and the 'informed' consent of various groups to merge their individual interests into a 'national' interest – and they start questioning the very basis of such consent given earlier, raise doubts regarding the form of government, express resentment over relative economic deprivation, demand self-determination or a greater role in the government or simply independence.

INTERNAL THREATS TO THE STABILITY OF THE COUNTRY FROM DIVISIVE MOVEMENTS

Indians love to proclaim that: "In spite of the diversities, India has managed to distil a national identity based on pluralism and secularism." How far this is true, is a matter of serious debate. We would avoid that. Yet, the fact remains that we have been talking about internal security more than anyone else in the whole world. We also project a siege mentality before others. We project an image of ourselves that is very fickle – as if the nation is so weakly bound that unless you clamp every single creak as tightly as you can, the whole edifice would fall apart in no time. If it is not so, we are making a fool of ourselves. If all that we talk about our problems is true in its entirety, then our prognosis is indeed very bad. The truth lies between the two extremes.

India's internal stability has come under increasing attack from various insurgencies, secessionist movements, sectarianism, religious strife and caste tensions – all of them threaten to rip apart the socio-political fabric of the nation. These include the **insurgency-cum-terrorism in Kashmir**, the **Maoist Naxal insurgency** in large parts of India, the **secessionist insurgencies** in several part of the **north-eastern States** of India, sporadic bursts of **terrorism** by certain elements amongst the Sikhs and Hindus, terrorism by certain elements amongst the Muslims, **communal clashes** (Hindu-Muslim, Hindu-Christian, etc) **caste clashes**, and **sectarian clashes** (such as Shia-Sunni). Internal security is such a major concern that the nation spends about one-fourth of its defence budget on internal security. A question must arise then – what is it that the nation is still holding out even as our handling of practically all these issues leaves much to be desired?

INDIA'S INTRINSIC ADVANTAGE OF A LARGE MOMENT OF INERTIA

If India gives the impression of being stable, what is the reason? Is it because of any intrinsic quality of India and the Indians? The answer is a categorical no! **That India has held together as a nation-State has more to do with the lack of certain qualities in its people rather than any qualities possessed**. We will analyse them shortly. Moment of inertia is a simple concept of physics. **Moment of inertia is a measure of stability under motion**. A flywheel, for example, has a large moment of inertia. Set it into motion and it will continue to rotate for a long time. In comparison, a ceiling fan has lesser moment of inertia. India's large moment of inertia comes from its sheer geographical size and the huge population. Smaller nations have smaller moments of inertia.

Why We could not Lose Kashmir and the North-Eastern States?

When insurgency started in Kashmir in 1988-89, it had a very strong insurrectional focus. It was almost an uprising against India. The end appeared to be round the corner – as if India could lose Kashmir anytime. One could feel the '**climate of collapse**' everywhere. Still, 28 years later also, Kashmir did not, could not break from India. In spite of all the violence, killings, bomb explosions and panic, India did not let Kashmir go. Why? It is because of India's large moment of inertia. Most people would not know that in 28 years, the security forces had lost 6,216 men in killed and nearly four times that in injured besides thousands of crores of rupees spent every year. Yet, the country was able to absorb that.

It was a miscalculation by those in the ISI who had armed and trained the Kashmiri terrorists. They did not factor in India's moment of inertia. The ISI had thought that the insurrectional focus would trigger a chain reaction amongst the people leading to the collapse of the regime. What they had not been able to do in 1947 from outside, they hoped to accomplish this time from within. **A smaller nation, with a smaller moment of inertia would have cracked under similar circumstances. That's why the Maoist insurgency had succeeded in Nepal and that's why a similar Maoist (Naxal) insurgency in India is not successful even after 48 years. India is, of course, not Nepal. India can afford to commit many mistakes and yet be able to absorb their consequences**.

The same thing happened with Nagaland and Manipur also. The insurgents did not understand that they could not militarily wrest these places from the Indian nation-State. It was too huge to be overcome.

OTHER FACTORS THAT HAVE CONTRIBUTED TO OUR SURVIVAL IN SPITE OF THE NATION'S INHERENT CONTRADICTIONS

The Indifferent Nature of the Indians

Moreover, the ISI also did not understand that India is essentially a very inert society. Indians do get highly excited; in fact their entire media survives and thrives on sensationalism. But their passions are short-lived. Their interest span is very short. However huge a tragedy be, they forget it in a few days and revert to their Bollywood songs and cricket routine. Indians are so selfish that unless something concerns them or their daily lives directly, they do not bother about it. Kashmir and the North-East happen to be on the fringes of India anyway. Even for Naxalism in the heart of India, incidents related to Naxalism are just another item in the papers or the TV channels. As a result, the problems in these areas could never really build up public pressure.

Indians are too selfish, too lazy, too inert, too indifferent, and too apathetic to really put their heart into any movement for a common cause. Precisely for this reason, insurgent movements in India suffer from a fundamental handicap. **In spite of all the contradictions in the Indian society; India drags on because Indians refuse to get involved in a mass movement for a common cause. India has held together as a nation-State more due to lack of certain qualities in the people rather than any qualities possessed by them.**

Historical Example of Indians' Apathy

It was due to the historic indifference of the Indian people that they were repeatedly subjugated by invaders. It is not that the invaders had such huge armies that every Indian could be subdued. Had they ever risen en masse, the invaders could have been driven away. They never revolted en masse. Why? They never revolted because they did not care. They did not care because they were absolutely apathetic to the fortune of the rulers who were, in any case, indifferent to the sufferings of the masses. The indifference of the rulers made the people into materialists, fatalists and above all, disinterested, disenchanted and apathetic to the affairs of those in power.

Opportunistic Nature of the People

The ISI also failed to read one important psychological aspect of the Indians – that people tend to be essentially opportunists. When the going was tough for the Government of India in the late '80s and early '90s, a large number of people in Kashmir were openly; blatantly anti-India, perhaps hoping that amidst all that confusion, subversion and violence, the Indian government would abdicate quite like Hari Singh. Unfortunately for them, the Government of India was not Hari Singh. It was not going to give up under any circumstance. When that hope of a quick 'collapse' receded, they were prepared to accept whatever that came along. That's how we were able to conduct the elections successfully in Kashmir in 1996 and consistently thereafter. Essentially, a similar thing has happened in more than one State of the North-East also. **In other words, insurgencies are not destined to succeed in India even as they can lead to a great deal of trouble for years. The country is surviving not because of any intrinsic strength of its own, but because of the intrinsic weaknesses of the disruptive forces.**

OTHER FACTORS THAT WEAKEN THE NATIONAL FABRIC

Lopsided Economic Development and Inequalities

India presents a study in stark contrasts. There are extremely wealthy people in India and, at the same time, there is massive poverty. Indian economy's growth story is a study in contrasts. In spite of the fabled Indian growth story and the fruits of economic liberalization; the growth, if at all there, has been there only for some very few. The fact is that paradoxes have nowhere been as stark as they are in modern India. Millions upon millions still sleep hungry; live in conditions worse than hovels; die untreated because they cannot afford the charges of the private hospitals; or simply commit suicide in sheer desperation. A frightening disparity exists in every walk of life; and there is great oppression all around at the hands of corrupt government servants.

Consequences for the Nation

Inequalities and injustice both produce deep resentment and unrest – at best, they make people indifferent and weaken their sense of belonging to the nation; at worst, they could make them hostile to the nation.

Lack of Innovative Capacity

India has sent rockets to the planet Mars. Yet, it has not designed a single car or even motorbike of world standard. They still dump practically all their sewerage in their rivers and have no system of waste disposal. The manufacturing sector of the country is hopelessly weak. **The national innovative capacity of India is exceptionally weak. The Indians have not designed anything. They are buyers, not makers**. Yes, the

Indians have an extremely large pool of technically qualified manpower, but that's only people who are technically qualified – that's all; nothing more. They are just not capable of thinking anything original by themselves. In the context of the famous IT industry, we call them 'software coolies'. Somebody else in the world invents and develops technologies – these guys merely use them and the Indians have the gall to call them professionals!

Their so-called centres of excellence in technical education have eventually been reduced to factories producing graduate engineer managers for the private sector. Not only that, they have not been able to create, invent or innovate anything even with the help of those who remain there to do their MTechs and PhDs. One must be intellectually honest to face it – what is the contribution of the IITs and other top Indian universities to world science or to anything that concerns the lives of the people in India? What innovation or invention owes its origin to the intellect of the Indians working in India? Nothing, just nothing.

In India, more than 17,000 drug formulations (and over 75,000 brands) are sold. How many of them have been invented in India? Not one, except a solitary Lipaglyn (Glitazar) invented in 2013 by Zydus! The Indians use TV sets, mobile phones, air conditioners, music systems, motorcycles, calculators, computers, cars by the millions upon millions – how many of them have been designed in India? Not one – TATA Indica/ Indigo and Nano are the only Indian cars designed in India in so many years! The remaining things are all manufactured on somebody else's design or creative intellectual effort. Kawasaki, Honda, Suzuki, Samsung, Motorola, Huawei; you name it –

they are all foreign designs. Most Indian companies proudly state in their advertisements that their products are made with the help of German/Japanese/Korean etc, technology and that actually boosts their brand value!

The real intellectual problem lies in creating, inventing or innovating something – that's where the Indians have failed summarily as a nation. They still remain a nation of coolies. Not only that the designs are made by someone else from tiny countries a fraction of the size of India, even the manufacturing of the products in India, if at all it takes place, is on imported machines – the Indians only work on those machines. All over India, Metro rails are projected as growth stories. By God, what is Indian in the Metro rails except the labour? The tunnel boring machines are imported; the heavy earth moving machines and cranes are imported; and even the Metro coaches are imported. **Other nations of the world strove hard to develop creative intellect; the Indians took pride in being able to purchase things invented and made by others**.

In mid-2015, NR Narayana Murthy, Chairman Emeritus, Infosys, was frank enough to bring it in public, "Have the institutions (in particular IISc and the Indian Institutes of Technology) over the past 60-plus years contributed to making our society and the world a better place? Is there one invention from India that has become a household name in the globe? The reality is that there is no such contribution from India in the last 60 years." Stung by this criticism, the chairman of the Scientific Advisory Council to the Prime Minister, Prof CNR Rao, slammed corporate India for 'pathetic' contribution towards science and education in the country. *The Indian Express*, in its editorial 'A Shared Failure', observed that both were right. **Fact is, both the centres of higher learning and the industry have failed India. There is no research in India worth its name in this country by anybody**.

Implications for National Security

This complex economic story has profound implications for national security. No nation can aspire to be a global power on the strength of virtually 100% imported weapon systems. A military propped up on massive imports may be good enough in a conventional war, to hold off or beat off a nation like Pakistan, and may be avert an ignominious defeat like 1962 at the hands of a nation like China. The dreams must end there.

THE STRENGTHS AND WEAKNESSES OF THE TERRORISTS AND INSURGENTS

A lot of speculation goes in the ignorant media about what exactly terrorists are capable of doing. The solitary successful 9/11 attack on the WTC Towers has fuelled this speculation. What they fail to understand is that 9/11 was strictly a one-off attack. It is not possible to repeat it. The possibility has been foreclosed with the adoption of stringent security measures at the airports. Unless there was some laxity or complicity, a repeat performance of 9/11 is rather unlikely.

Terrorists might be able to make Radiological Dispersal Devices or the so-called Dirty Bombs but they would not be effective. They can try to make biological weapons too by a careful exploitation of **dual use technologies**. But they would still be capable of killing a few people only – like the Aum Shinrikyo attack. Since the so-called self-styled experts and the media do not have any understanding of the complex phenomenon of terrorism in all its dimensions, they fail to see through the fact that the real strength of the terrorist does not lie in his ability to inflict great material damage. He needs to inflict some damage because unless he does that, he would not be taken seriously. And he can do that with the nearly 70 year old AK-47 rifles also. He can do that sitting on his laptop also by launching cyber attacks and that requires a different preparation altogether to prevent or combat it. He does not really need nuclear bombs, chemical and biological weapons. **The greatest strength of the terrorist lies in his being an amorphous, ubiquitous and invisible entity that does not present a clear, well-defined target and which can strike anywhere in the most unpredictable manner. The moment he ceases to be so, he is easy meat for the conventional military power of nation-States**.

Liberation Tigers of Tamil Eelam (LTTE)

The LTTE was great as a terrorist organization with some of the most spectacular, most efficiently executed terrorist strikes in the world executed by them. The Sri Lankan security machinery was absolutely at a loss to figure out how to deal with them. Yet, the moment they decided to hold and administer territory in northern Sri Lanka, they provided a tangible target for the conventional forces of Sri Lanka and were all killed to the last man – utterly destroyed.

Jarnail Singh Bhindaranwale

Earlier, Jarnail Singh Bhindaranwale had committed the same mistake in India. Had he not committed the mistake of hiding in the Golden Temple, Khalistani terrorism could have easily gone on for years. By hiding there and mistakenly thinking that the religious place is inviolable, he presented a tangible target to the Indian security forces and was destroyed.

Taliban

The Taliban in Afghanistan had committed the same mistake after their, ironically, US-aided victorious war against the Soviets. By taking over the government, they presented a clear target to the US when it turned against them. Having been thrown out of power after the 2001 attacks, they realized their mistake and once again became an amorphous, ubiquitous and invisible entity – sometimes hiding in the hills or other remote, inaccessible areas; sometimes mingling with the villagers. The US tried everything they could – boots on the ground; drone strikes; bombardment; you name it; they had tried it and spent nearly $ 715 billion on it till September 2015. In the end, they completely failed to destroy the Taliban and were rather forced to hold secret parleys with them. But in September 2015, the Taliban were found repeating their earlier mistake. They attacked and captured the city of Kunduz, albeit for a while. Once again, they forgot that now they present an identifiable target. The whole cycle will get repeated.

Islamic State of Iraq and Syria (ISIS)

The ISIS is found committing the same mistake. Yes, it indeed gives a primitive high to capture places, rule them and commit atrocities upon prisoners – the sense of having total power over some people works like an aphrodisiac. But once again, they do not know what the US airpower can do to them in just one day. If they continue to hold territory, they are going to be destroyed. They cannot fight like conventional forces on the strength of light weaponry obtained from the illegal arms bazaar and without any defence industrial base of their own. In the end, unless they correct this fundamental mistake, they stand to get destroyed someday by superior forces.

Al Qaida

The Al Qaida has never committed this mistake and that's how it survives till date, despite the US dropping bombs on every stupid hillock and field in Afghanistan for 14 years and despite their having wasted some $ 819 billion in military operations in Iraq since 1991. They are not holding any territory anywhere in the world and are found literally everywhere.

Intelligent terrorists would fight the minds of their adversaries; not their military hardware! One who understands this will be successful; others will be decimated.

POSSIBLE 'DRIVERS' AND SITUATIONS OF DISINTEGRATION OF THE NATION-STATE

Thus at the moment, India is able to avoid disintegration because it is enjoying a dynamic equilibrium between its massive inertia which resists any change and the fissiparous tendencies, which are the 'drivers' of disintegration. This is a rather delicate balance and can indeed tilt towards fragmentation too under suitable circumstances. It will be like what is known in metallurgical engineering as 'metal fatigue' – a piece of metal which is subjected to repeated stress, suddenly gives way. It will be like one tear in a fabric which grows to rip it apart. Now what those circumstances could be? Some illustrative drivers and situations or circumstances which could widen the cracks are discussed below. The list is not exhaustive.

Military Reverses

For one, military reverses suffered in a particular part of the country could be such a driver. If India, for example, suffers military reverses in Kashmir or in the North-East the opportunists will mobilize quickly; and the combined effect of the two could very well revive insurgency to such an extent that it ushers in the dreaded 'climate of collapse'. **The reverses must come first; the insurgent strikes must follow them so as to accentuate the effect of the former. The insurgents could indulge in some clever fifth-columnist action also. That would be a real force multiplier for them. Pakistan has repeatedly failed in their ventures of using tribal raiders/mujahideen against India in the wars of 1947, 1965 and again in 1999 because they have been trying the other way round – they did not inflict any military reverses first and yet thought that the insurgencies instigated by them would generate their own momentum**.

Disruption of Command Structure

A nuclear strike at the nerve centre of the country, for example, leading to paralysis of the governing structure of the country, and perhaps a surrender (as envisaged by Humphrey Hawksley in *Dragon Fire*), could be another driver as it would generate widespread despondency and frustration with the regime.

Damage to Critical Infrastructure

Widespread destruction of critical infrastructure or important industries in war or as a result of sabotage by insurgents or enemy strikes could be another driver because the Indians, having never been baptized by 'blood and fire' in wars, are not as used to suffering as many nations of the world have been.

They may blame the regime for their sufferings and seek some radical changes.

Sustained Terrorism

Terrorism, if skilfully applied on a soft State could be yet another driver. Skilful application of terrorism means that they have to select their targets carefully for maximum psychological impact in the minds of the people that matter. The Indian society and its irresponsible media have developed a morbid fear of violence and the great middle-class reacts to it in a most irrational manner. This has made the Indian society particularly vulnerable to acts of terrorism – intelligent terrorists can certainly extort more out of the Indian State than they can ever expect from a principled and resolute State.

Paralysing of Key Institutions

Terrorizing the key institutions of the government and thus bringing about a paralysis in the functioning of the administration is also a potent driver with manifold results possible. If the police or the security forces are the target, terror can cause a sort of disillusionment to set in, leading them to a state of shock and inactivity. Conversely, if the government persists in trying to stamp out terrorism under the pressure of the people and the media, the resources of the police and the army would be greatly stretched, making them even less effective.

Financial Pressure

Terrorism or insurgencies may also lead to a heavy financial burden on the system as extra security measures require to be put in place.

Media and Public Pressure

Under the pressure of relentless terrorist attacks or insurgent violence coupled with their sensationalization in the media, there could be a clamouring from a large section of the people, the media and even the ruling group for what they perceive as a panacea in the days of participative democracies, that is, a dialogue. A dialogue would be essentially nothing but a tacit admission that the regime has buckled up and is prepared to grant some concessions. It is for India and Indians to avoid becoming a soft State.

IMPERATIVES AND SOLUTIONS FOR CONTINUED SURVIVAL

It is not that the problems of India cannot be solved ever. People of other lands did learn to place something above their parochial considerations and moved on with the process of nation-building. Still, the people alone will have to decide what they value more – their small-group identity crises or collective interests as a subset of a larger set. We will have to drive this point home, instead of indulging in juvenile rhetoric. The true spirit of nationalism is not something which can be inculcated by exhortations and harangues – it is a realization that should spring from within. Then, we, as a nation, will have to clearly recognize the fissiparous tendencies inherent in our system and be on guard against all the possible 'drivers' and situations which can lead to the disintegration of the country.

3

Fifty Years of Naxalism in India

Dr PK Agrawal

Naxalism has been the gravest problem to the internal security in India. More people have been killed in violence by Naxalites than the causalities in terror related violence in Jammu and Kashmir and insurgency in the north-eastern States.

The Naxalite movement started from Naxalbari in Siliguri Subdivision of Darjeeling district of West Bengal in 1967, after twenty years of independence of India. Its flames have spread to many parts of the country. A day does not pass when an incident of violence by Naxalites or counter violence by police force is not reported in newspapers or viewed on the silver screen.

It is also called the 'red terror'. Ajit Doval, former Director of the Intelligence Bureau (IB) and now India's National Security Adviser stated that Naxal activities affect approximately 40% of the country's land mass and at least 35% of the total population. It started from West Bengal in 1967 but has now extended to States of Chhattisgarh, Madhya Pradesh,

Jharkhand, Odisha, Andhra Pradesh, Bihar, Maharashtra, Karnataka and Uttar Pradesh.

Before we go through the gradual spread of the Naxalite movement especially in rural areas, we should agree that where there is injustice, violence will be its natural fall out. If an equitable or egalitarian society is established in true sense, there will be peace. The equity can be achieved either by liberal releases of funds, goods or services by the government or by equitable redistribution of properties by the State. In rural India, most of the properties are locked in landed properties. Therefore, equitable distribution of land through various Zamindari abolition and land reforms statutes was focused just after the independence of the country in the year 1947. However, the initial enthusiasm gradually steamed off as the political executives became *pro status quo* and did not exert themselves for revolutionary changes in favour of the landless poor and share-croppers in rural India.

NAXALBARI FLARE-UP AND ITS SPREAD

The movement started when CPI(M) leaders who followed Karl Marx, decided to enter the Government in West Bengal after General Election in 1967. The revolutionary section who swear by Mao Tse-tung's political thought resented it for they thought violent revolution is the only way to capture power. The tribal population of 1,26,000 led by late Charu Mazumdar, Secretary General, Communist Party of India (Marxist-Leninist) (CPI-ML) on 3rd March 1967 forcibly seized land and killed number of landlords as class enemies including government officials. Few revenue officers close to landlords were injured and beheaded and their houses gutted.

Their legs and hands were fractured and nose cut off. They demonstrated to other government officials that they should not indulge in corruption and should not compromise with landlords at the cost of poor farmers.

The second in command Kanu Sanyal raised armed struggle through Peasants Committee in Naxalbari during 1967 (March-April) to get recorded share croppers known as Bargadars in West Bengal and was quite successful to raise the issue in the country. Naxalite movement found good takers in Bihar right from April 1968 in Mushahari in Muzaffarpur district because injustice prevailing was writ large in Bihar. Scandal after scandal and the stink of corruption provided breeding ground for the Naxalite movement in Bihar and it soon spread its wings to contiguous districts of Rohtas, Singhbhum (now in Jharkhand), Gaya, Aurangabad and Bhojpur.

There was a gruesome massacre in Pipri which triggered off violence in Belchhi, where on May 27, 1977, Kurmis, a backward caste local group, killed 11 Chamars (Dalits) in land dispute which shook the conscience of the nation and late Indira Gandhi visited there. Similarly, one Harijan or Dalit boy in Kanchi Kancharla in Andhra Pradesh was burnt alive for stealing brass utensils. Then followed a rash of violent incidents in Kilavemani in Tamil Nadu where 25 Harijans were burnt alive in Villupurami. Many areas of Marathwada following the Dalit Panther agitations caused a lot of ripples in Maharashtra.

The Police hobnobbed with landowners and lack of firm land records provided fuel to the fire. The Naxalites became active in tri-junction areas of Odisha, Andhra Pradesh and

Chhattisgarh (mainly erstwhile Bastar district). The largest and the most backward district of Bastar having tribals as majority population, found readymade support among the tribals. In Bastar (now Bijapur, Narayanpur and Dantewara districts), the tribals were not only poor without proper land entitlements, they were also exploited by the outsides and were neglected by the local government officials and even by local panchayats.

However, the Naxalites found easy shelter, in bordering areas of two States so that they can flee away after committing crimes like in tri-junction areas of tri-junction Jharkhand, Odisha adjoining East Madanpur district of West Bengal. After the collapse of the Naxalite movement in Mushahari (Muzaffarpur) and the Wynand jungles in Kerala, the village Chauri in Bhojpur district of south-west Bihar caught the media headlines on May 6, 1973. After collapse of the United Front Ministry, the Congress Party came into power headed by Siddhartha Shankar Ray who crushed the Naxalite movement by personally supervising the State violence with strong hand and determination taking full responsibility on his own. Thousands of suspected young Naxalites and their supporters were arrested by police, tortured and killed in fake encounters by police without bothering violation of Human Rights. Victory in 1971 War with Pakistan and liberation of Bangladesh in the Eastern Sector made Ray the most powerful Chief Minister. Later on he was inducted by Indira Gandhi at the Centre to declare emergency in 1975 and committed excessive on national scale. However, his expertise was later on best utilized by the Congress Party regime to crush terrorism in Punjab as Governor of Punjab. Though, the Naxalite movement was crushed here and there but it reappeared elsewhere in a bigger way and became a permanent feature of the Indian polity for times to come.

CONSOLIDATION PHASE OF NAXALISM

The various factions of Naxalites, consolidated and united themselves to fight against the onslaught of police force on them and merciless torturing of their cadres and supporters. The main front (CPI-ML) People's War Group ie PWG was formed on Lenin's birth anniversary on April 22, 1980. Kondapalli Seetharamaiah one of the most influential Naxalite leaders from Andhra Pradesh and a member of the erstwhile Central Organizing Committee of the Communist Party of India Marxist-Leninist (CPI-ML) is the founding father of the PWG. The other faction CPI-ML Liberation advocated for participation in elections and other democratic processes. The CPI-ML Liberation recorded its first electoral victory under the banner of the IPF (Indian People's Front) in 1989 and Arrah, Lok Sabha constituency in Central Bihar sent the first 'Naxalite' as member to Parliament. Gradually, to save from police onslaught Liberation's way of movement became weak and the PWG's operations started gaining momentum.

MCC also started merging with PWG in 1981. However continuity of leadership and split in the Central Committee (CC) delayed the unity process for several years.

In the meantime, many Left Wing Extremist (LWE) groups appeared on the scene operating with a lot of underground and overground cadres and supporters. The CPM-People's War Group (53%) and Maoist Communist Centre (MCC) (30%) continue to spearhead LWE violence respectively.

The basic thrust of different outfits of Naxalites is to focus attention on the grievances of the people, inequalities suffered by large segments of the population, release of victims of exploitation from the tentacles of the landlords, etc and to inculcate class responsibilities among the economically and socially deprived sections of society. In pursuance of these objectives, the groups have not only mobilized the people but have also ensured that distributive justice is available in a rough and ready manner. The people's courts organized by these groups expropriate surplus land from the landlords as per ceiling laws to be distributed among the landless, dispense criminal justice, settle disputes and punish offenders. Thus, 'Jan Adalats' constitute a corner stone of their efforts to win over the masses particularly in the rural areas. Besides they indulge in extortion from businessmen, contractors, traders, government officers etc and resort to kidnapping and murders to eliminate interference by agents of the established and defiant class enemies.

Similarly, in the forest areas of Andhra Pradesh, Chhattisgarh, the Vidarbha region of Maharashtra, Odisha and Jharkhand, the Naxalites have led the tribals to occupy forest lands that they should have enjoyed in the normal course of things under their traditionally recognized rights, but which were denied and harassed by the government officials while the government remained indifferent to the need for paying minimum wages to the Adivasi (tribal) Tendu leaf gatherers in Andhra Pradesh and Madhya Pradesh. The Naxalites by launching a movement have secured increase in the rate payment for the picking.

The practice of forced labour (*begar*) in Andhra Pradesh under which the toiling caste had to provide free labour to the upper castes in violation of Article 17 of the Constitution, was done away with due to major upsurge by the Naxalites in the late 1970, and early 1980s of the last century.[1]

The movement did not bring any immediate results and was wound up by 1980. But it had far reaching implications and became a forces behind numerous peasant struggles in different areas of West Bengal, Bihar, Jharkhand (by tribals) Chhattisgarh (by tribals) Andhra Pradesh and Punjab. Though the CPI(M) and other left parties like Forward Bloc and RSP did not support the Naxalite movement in West Bengal yet they were in agreement with demand of Naxalites that land reform needs of the poorest of the poor in rural areas should be met on top priority basis. The Left Front Government led by CPI(M) in its three successive terms starting from 1977 salvaged the situation by recording fifteen lakh share-croppers or Bargadars under 'Barga operation' and distributed government surplus lands to about 14 lakh beneficiaries i e landless and the marginal farmers. This gave basic stability to the Left Front Government rule in West Bengal for more than thirty years before they were overthrown due to indulgence in corruption by grass root functionaries of block administration and Panchayat functionaries neglecting the implementation of land reforms which is a continuous process.

Naxalism continued and resurfaced here and there in nineteen nineties with more vigour and better organizational capability in other parts of India.

The violence figures for four years are as follows:

TABLE 1

	Total Incidents	*Deaths*
1990	1,570	413
1991	1,876	474
1992	1,337	503
1993	1,277	470

It covered about 80 million landless people and 30 million tribals. It was still considered as demand centric movement of the rural poor who deserved a better deal from the State. It was only at the start of the twenty first century that it had assumed a serious threat to the internal security scenario as violence and the killings by Naxalites exceeded violence and murders by terror groups in Punjab, North-East and Jammu and Kashmir and local police felt helpless and Central Security Forces had to be deployed to tackle violence by Naxalites.

DECLINE PHASE OF NAXALITE MOVEMENT

The Naxalite movement which started to fulfil the basic needs of the rural poor became an outfit fighting a pitched battle with the police for its existence. Figures published by the Ministry of Home Affairs, Government of India from 2003 to 2008 (6 years)[2] show that the incidents of Naxal violence were increasing involving more causalities as shown in Table 2.

TABLE 2

	Total (6 years)	*Average per year*
Number of incidents	9,403	1,567
Number of Casualties in civilians	2,871	479
Number of Causalities in Security forces	982	164
Number of Naxalite killed	892	149

Between 2003 to 2006, 4,890 Naxalites surrendered before the police. In 2001, there were, 1,208 violent incidents and 564 killings, and in 2002, there were 1,465 incidents involving 482 killings. The average of incidents and deaths from year 2010 to the year 2014 are 1,904 and 684 respectively showing that though incidents are increasing yet due to better police action, number of deaths is on decline from 792.

It is only from the beginning of 2015, the Naxal violence is on the decline as regards total casualties. "The movement today is in a very fragmented state. There are about forty odd groups operating under various labels in different parts of the country. Ten of them could be considered active. These are the People's War Group, Maoist Communist Centre, CPI-ML Liberation Group, CPI-ML Party Unity, CPI-ML K Ramachandran faction, CPI-ML Phani Bagchi Group, CPI-ML Yatindra Kumar Group, Kerala Communist Party, CPI-ML Red Flag and Communist Organization of India (ML). The first four have sizeable following and are conspicuously violence prone."[3]

According to an estimate by Prakash Singh, the total membership of all the Naxal groups of various shades is around fifty thousand. It should be much more now. To run their large organizational structure, they extort money from the landowners, moneyed men and contractors. They execute their action in the following four phases.

(i) Identify the area.

(ii) Develop contact with the local people of that area to make them their supporters.

(iii) Commit serious offences by forming groups.

(iv) Form the liberated zone.

In the liberated zone, they run parallel administration. They are well aware of the terrain and impose maximum casualties on paramilitary forces. The Naxal groups are experts in laying the mines as the area is in their control.

As per the report appearing in *The Telegraph* (Kolkata, dated 23rd May 2008), the Maoists have widened their network three fold in the past two years, spreading to 183 districts from 55 in 2005 across 16 States."[4] In fact, full Naxal affected districts are 76 only in India as on date. The number of districts affected by Naxal menace is on gradual decline. Some States have innovative measures, like Andhra Pradesh which has founded the anti-Naxal police force known as Grey Hounds team or squads. This team or force is adept in jungle warfare, though this force had initial casualty of more than 37 of its men, yet it has proved very effective and "there has been a decline of 40% in Maoist violence activities since its formation by the Andhra Pradesh Government.[5] Similarly, Chhattisgarh government had adopted an innovative method of tackling Naxalites by forming Salva Judum groups in Bastar region in June 2005. Salva Judum activists mobilized people against Naxalites through a series of rallies, meetings and padyatra's (rallies) in Naxal strongholds of Dantewada and Bijapur districts in south Bastar. Naxalites attacked the Salva Judum activists. After killing of its leader in a big blast with many Congress leaders, the Salva Judum movement has declined. However, Chhattisgarh Government is experimenting the posting of Special Police Officers (SPOs) on the pattern of Jammu zone to tackle terrorism. The performance of SPOs along-with the village Defence Committees has been commendable to support security forces to provide information and help in operation. They also infuse confidence among villagers that they may not fully succumb to pressures by Naxalites to support them. However, the morale of police has to be strengthened. The officers have to lead from the front like in the Indian army. Trained new outfit of police and para military forces in jungle and guerilla warfare will have to be created like the mountain divisions in the army. Training in jungle and guerilla warfare will have to be imparted to the existing units of police and para military forces posted in Naxal affected areas.

GOVERNMENT APPROACH TO TACKLE NAXALISM

The Union Government in the Ministry of Home Affairs and concerned State Governments have well laid down policy to tackle and liquidate Naxalism. The NDA government under the Prime Minister Narendra Modi defines Naxalism as Left Wing Extremism (LWE) on the basis of their ideology as distinct from earlier UPA government led by Congress.

The Central Government has adopted an integrated four points approach to address the Naxal problem in the areas of security, development, enforcing rights and entitlements of local communities, public perception management and good governance.

The common strategy of both governments to deal with the problem of Naxalism has the following main features:

1. The Centre will fund the Naxal-affected States for modernization of the State police for sophisticated and latest telecommunication equipments and network by construction of more mobile towers and sophisticated weaponry if not superior to the weaponry used by the Naxalites in the vulnerable police stations.
2. **The Centre has undertaken to reimburse recurring security related expenditure (SRE)** on rehabilitation and resettlement of Naxalite cadres, community policing, expenditure on village defence communities like Salwa Judum in Bastar, Chhattisgarh. Central Government also reimburses expenditure incurred on publicity to counter propaganda perpetuated by Naxalites and to seek cooperation from the civil society and the media.
3. **Additional Central Assistance (ACA)** has been earmarked to Naxal-affected districts to improve public infrastructure and services in Naxal-affected areas like construction of school buildings, school furniture, Anganwadi centres, drinking water facilities, rural roads, Panchayat Bhawans/community halls, godowns/ PDS shops, livelihood activities, skill development/ training, minor irrigation works, electric lighting, health centre facilities, Ashram Schools, construction of toilets, construction of multi-purpose Chaupals,

construction of passenger waiting halls, special coaching classes for students, construction of ANM Centres, development of playgrounds etc. There is hardly any development issue which is left out. Only tardy implementation has to be made speedy and foolproof and which is the entire responsibility of the State Governments.

4. **Road Requirement Plan (RRP)** has been approved for improvement of road connectivity in 34 extremely Naxal-affected districts in States viz, Andhra Pradesh, Bihar, Chhattisgarh, Jharkhand, Madhya Pradesh, Maharashtra, Odisha and Uttar Pradesh. This will meet the often repeated complaint by the security forces regarding problems faced by them in their mobility due to lack of roads in their campaign against Naxalites.
5. The Centre has sanctioned 400 new fortified police stations in Naxal-affected States at a cost of ₹2 crore each. Two hundred of them have already been constructed.
6. Distribution of title of the land to the tribals in the fringe areas of the forests where they have been residing for generations under the Scheduled Tribe and other Traditional Forest Dwellers (Recognition of Forest Rights) Act, 2006 in Naxal-affected areas on priority. Projects for development of social and physical infrastructure up to 1 hectare has been approved for non-forest purposes. The progress is very slow in this regard. Up-gradation of Kutcha road constructed prior to 1st September 1980 has also been approved. Both governments also professed for speedy implementation

of the Panchayats (Extension to Scheduled Areas) Act (PESA), 1986 to ensure *inter alia* that tribals can access to minor forest produce.

7. **Monitoring Mechanism:** The Indian administration has been leading in the world in regard to monitoring mechanism. In case of Naxal problem, the mechanism is perfect in three tiers:
   (i) There is a Standing Committee of the Chief Ministers of the Naxal-affected States under the Chairmanship of the Union Home Minister for periodic review of policy and measures on the political, security and development fronts.
   (ii) Review Group under the Cabinet Secretary to review quarterly developmental and security related works with the concerned central Government Secretaries, Chief Secretaries and Director General of Police of affected States.
   (iii) Monthly review by the concerned Chief Secretary of the concerned State with the DGP and Secretaries of development departments of the States. Joint Secretary from the Home Ministry may attend these reviews in the States."[6]

A NEW APPROACH

The report[1] 'Development Challenges in Extremist Affected Areas' authored by an expert group set up by the Planning Commission, looks at the Naxalite/Maoist movement in a way that is different from the prevalent official attitude and draws attention to many of the positive effects of the movement. The report rejects the official 'Security Centric' approach in dealing with the movement and instead suggests an ameliorative approach with emphasis on a negotiated solution.

The expert group headed by D Bandyopadhyay of 'Operation Barga' fame in West Bengal, lays stress on the 'Structural violence' which is implicit in the social and economic system and which in the opinion of its authors prompts the radical groups to justify their own violent acts.

IMPLEMENTATION OF LAND REFORMS AS THE PERMANENT SOLUTION OF NAXALISM

Naxalites nowadays are only engaged in countering the powerful State police force and they have been virtually left with no time or opportunity to follow to their main agenda to ensure land to the landless, the tiller, delivery of justice to the poor, etc.

> "If government surplus land is not available for distribution, the government should purchase land in the same village or neighbouring village where the landless poorest of the poor will go and cultivate the land and will save himself and his family from starvation. The government should distribute minimum 16 decimals per family for three tier cultivation starting from coarse grain cultivation and vegetable cash crops to fast growing trees as in Bangladesh."[7]

In Jharkhand, government surplus ceiling and land should be distributed among the landless persons, specially the tribals on priority. In Chhattisgarh, all lands including unsurveyed land of Abujmarh area in erstwhile Bastar district covering more than 5,000 hectares should be surveyed and updated. Computerized land records should be made and distributed to all landowners and pattadars. In the State of Odisha, bataidars (sharecroppers) should be recorded on lands which have been cultivated by them on the promise or by convention to share produce. In Madhya Pradesh, the tribals living on the fringe of forests should be recorded and given the right to collect minor forest produce or dry leaves under the STORFA, 2006. Karnataka presents a scenario, where contact farming can be utilized for the advantage of the farmers whose lands have been given for contract farming.

Uttar Pradesh highlights a scene where land acquired for large public sector enterprises is still lying vacant and is a source of problem for the units as well as for local people.

In Andhra Pradesh, land is required to be restored to the tribals which was illegally transferred to non-tribals. In Andhra Pradesh, Nyaya Panchayats at the block level or at the level of Panchayat Samitis is an innovation worth emulation by other States. In Bihar, land records are almost non-existent, in spite of availability of requisite funds from the Central Government for the purpose. There is an urgent need for updating of land records and vesting of surplus lands in government belonging to erstwhile zamindars or jotedars.

In West Bengal, a large quantum of land is locked in court cases especially at the High Court and the Supreme Court which can be distributed, if released from Courts, among the landless poor. In Maharashtra, lack of bank finance for the crops is the main cause of suicides by the farmers especially in the Vidarbha regions of Maharashtra.

The police solution is underway in all affected States of India. There are some stories of success of the police operation like Grey Hounds in Andhra Pradesh, Auxiliary Armed Police Force in Chhattisgarh, killing of top Naxalite leader in a genuine police encounter in West Bengal, 40% recruitment in Central paramilitary forces from border areas and areas affected by militancy or Naxalism. However, due 'political will' to solve the Naxalism problem, by the State Governments has not yet been demonstrated.

CONCLUSION

Due to traditional anti-people working of police, the police action could not make perceptible change in the situation. There is more of blame game between the local police and deployed paramilitary forces, posting of unwilling officers in those areas rather than the cream of officers from the State police force, incidents of connivance of local police with Naxalites and lack of actionable intelligence information by local police set-ups and inadequate bank of knowledge about local inhospitable terrain with the local police. Even if all deficiencies are removed in the police set-up, it will not be able to solve the problem unless concerted efforts are made through implementation of land reform measures and development schemes in an impartial manner. Development schemes afflicted with corruption fuel the Naxalite agitation more than they solve. But development schemes cannot be stopped for that reason. There should be many times more vigilance on execution of developmental schemes in Naxal affected areas than elsewhere in the country. I am sure that the Indian administration led by political executives will awake and undertake implementation of land reform measures in the Naxal affected States on top priority basis.

REFERENCES

1. Planning Commission of India: Report titled 'Development Challenges in Extremist Affected Areas' by an Expert Group, *EPW*, May 24-30, 2008, pp 11 and 12.
2. Website www.mha.nic.in as on 19th August 2015.
3. Singh, Prakash: *The Naxalite Movement in India*, 1995, Rupa & Co, New Delhi, pp 139-40.
4. *The Telegraph*, Kolkata 23rd May 2008 under title, 'Red Run – 7 to 16 States in Two Years', published by AB Group of Newspapers, Kolkata.
5. Uday Kumar: *Defeating Naxalite*, 2012, Lucky International, New Delhi, p 49.
6. Agrawal, Dr PK: *Solution to Naxalism*, 2016, Manas Publications, New Delhi, pp 25-29.
7. *Business Economics*, Fortnightly Magazine, Chief Editor: Karnoria, HP, 16-30 November 2015, pp 32-33, Kolkata.

4

Civil-Military Divide

Sunil S Parihar

> Nations which fail to develop a balanced pattern of civil-military relations squander their resources and run uncalculated risks.
>
> – Admiral Vishnu Bhagwat

The rift between India's bureaucracy and military is now out in the open, though it started soon after India got its independence. The Defence Secretary, who till then had a limited role of pushing files and signing documents on behalf of the government, became all powerful as staff officer of the Defence Minister, who was given control of the country's defence services. In a democracy there has to be 'civil' control over military of course, but in every democracy world over, the word 'civil' implies political and not bureaucratic control. In India, our political leadership over the years has generally excluded the military leadership from decision making process in higher defence management. This trend was started by India's first Prime Minister Jawaharlal Nehru. In the famous, or rather infamous, Krishna Menon – Gen KS Thimayya episode, Nehru sided with Menon, his Defence Minister, and manipulated things in such a manner, that the General had to resign.

Veteran journalist Inder Malhotra ('Khaki versus Khadi', *The Indian Express*, 17 October 2008), describes the event thus: "S Gopal (Nehru's biographer) perceived the Thimayya-Menon episode as 'a comic-opera putsch'. According to him, Nehru dealt with it in Parliament "in such a way as to strengthen Menon's position and shrink Thimayya's reputation. He stressed the importance of the government's control of the armed forces and hinted that Thimayya had acted irresponsibly." Snubbing the General and by extension the armed forces, may have given some ego boost to both Nehru and Menon, but four years later the nation paid the price for their undue interference in matters military in the form of the Himalayan Blunder of 1962. It is pertinent to point out, that several heads did roll after the debacle but the bureaucrats dealing with the country's defence affairs got away without a scratch, even as Nehru wrote,

> "I think it was Voltaire who defined the 'Holy Roman Empire' as something which was neither holy, nor Roman, nor an empire. Just as someone else once defined the Indian Civil Service, with which we are unfortunately still afflicted in this country, as neither Indian, nor civil, nor a service."

Things haven't changed much ever since and in fact have gone from bad to worse. The bureaucrats' stranglehold over higher defence management has ensured that the generals are kept on the periphery, from where they can neither influence the decision making process nor protest over being excluded. All powers, organizational, financial and promotional, are concentrated in the hands of the bureaucrats at the MoD. The Defence Secretary and even the Joint Secretaries can walk into the office of the Defence Minister anytime whereas the Service Chiefs generally get to meet the Defence Minister only during weekly meetings. General S Padmanabhan in his book *A General Speaks*, had this to say about meeting of Service Chiefs with the Defence Minister:

> "Even at the level of the Defence Minister and Service Chiefs, exchanges on major matters of defence policy were few and far between, the Defence Minister's weekly meetings with the Service Chiefs being used to update the minister and equip him to negotiate questions in Parliament. Often, these meetings were deferred, as 'more important' activities claimed the time of the minister.... The result was ... the greater role and authority assumed by the Defence bureaucracy. The Defence Secretary, with his nearness to the Defence Minister, often began to exercise power on the minister's behalf and was, quite often, regarded as de facto defence minister. The 'supremacy of the civil over the military' was thus effectively changed from supremacy of the political authority to that of the civilian bureaucracy."

Bureaucrats continue to run down the Defence Services with great zeal. With successive Central Pay Commissions they have ensured that the status of armed forces goes down while they themselves get upgraded. Why the military has never been represented in the pay commission? It's perhaps bureaucrats' way of adding insult to injury. Bureaucrats apart, their political bosses haven't really cared either. The 'supposedly nationalist'

BJP-led NDA government at the Centre was expected to restore the status of the armed forces, but unfortunately, this has not happened. In fact, they seem to be doing more harm than good and adding to the woes and angst of the soldiers. The 7th Pay Commission has been no different than the earlier ones, as far as the defence personnel are concerned; they have once again been discriminated against and left out in the cold. While the bureaucrats have been at it for long, essentially to impose their supremacy over defence services in the guise of civilian control, the question is why politicians side with them rather than those in uniform? After all, helping the soldiers' cause will make them look good in the eyes of people – read voters – in general, besides the substantial 'Fauji' vote at stake anyway. Is it because they are apprehensive of a coup if the military is not kept in check? Given the apolitical nature of the services and their past track record, it would be ridiculous to think that way. But then the bureaucrats have at times tried to scare the political establishment with the bogey of military take over, so one never knows. What's more likely, however, is the fact that the Netas and Babus enjoy a mutually beneficial relationship and scratch each other's back.

Another reason could be plain envy, as brought out by Lt Gen PC Katoch, ex-Special Forces. He says,

> "While very few have been able to explain the real reason behind the antipathy against the military displayed by the civil bureaucracy and the political executive, my experience suggests that non-military personnel perhaps resent the armed forces because of their evidently orderly and efficient ethos, the tightly bound camaraderie and distinct standing in the society. And this is not unique to India."

Renowned sociologist Morris Janowitz had famously said:

> "The intimate social solidarity of the military profession is both envied and resented by civilians."

Whatever be the reasons, the fact of the matter is that the civil-military relations in India today, are at an all time low. And that's a very serious issue, as far as the national security is concerned.

The politicians are pretty much aware of what ails India's higher defence structures. Rajeev Chandrashekhar, Independent MP, an expert on matters military and member of Parliament standing committee on defence, not only supports reforms recommended by various committees but has often expressed his displeasure over non-implementation of the same by the MoD. In 2007, a standing committee report, on the CDS, said that "the Government should take the GoM (Group of Ministers) recommendations as well as this Committee's concern in this matter seriously and take the final decision on CDS at the earliest." In 2009, another Standing Committee on Defence (SCD) said that it is "of the considered view that the creation of an additional post of Chief of Defence Staff (CDS) to act as Chairman of the CoSC (Chiefs of Staff Committee) is essential to ensure optimum level of jointness among different wings of the Armed Forces and to provide single-point military advice to the Government." Parliamentary committees have also been critical of the Defence Ministry's unwillingness to implement the required reforms. The second SCD report of the 15th Lok Sabha mentioned:

> "Merely writing letters even from the level of the Defence Minister is not sufficient. There is an urgent need to use

> various fora of interaction with the leaders of the political parties.... The Committee expects the Ministry to take the effective steps as suggested above so that the institution of CDS is set up expeditiously."

Veteran Lt Gen SK Sinha, in an article "Man on the Horseback" (*Asian Age*) observed,

> "India is the only country in the world without a Chief of Defence Staff or equivalent and with a MoD working on a 'we and they' syndrome, rather than an 'us' outlook. This gravely undermines our Defence preparedness and our ability to face the current very serious national security challenges."

While the proposal of appointing CDS and other reforms have been kept in cold storage by the manipulative bureaucrats without much resistance from the military leadership, the push now seems to have turned into a shove. In an unprecedented move, the Chiefs of the three services have refused to implement the 7th CPC notification, and have jointly asked the government to first remove grave anomalies that have been pointed out on several occasions but remain unchanged. At the time of writing this, the situation is pretty fluid and grave. The Defence Minister has asked the service chiefs to start implementing the benefits of the 7th Pay Commission to the troops and assured that the anomalies that have been brought out will be resolved as soon as possible. Meanwhile, the social media is abuzz with various conspiracy theories and views with many retired Generals giving vent to their hitherto suppressed feelings. Some Politicians from the opposition parties are adding fuel to fire. Bureaucrats, the main actors, seem to be merrily enjoying the drama from the wings as usual, and in all probability, the military leadership of our not so friendly neighbours would be doing the same.

The political leadership must realize that it's actually a watershed moment in the country's history of civil-military relations. They need to act and act fast. Unlike protests over OROP where it was mainly the veterans who were at the fore front and as such could be taken lightly, it's the serving soldiers now who are unhappy with the government's apathy towards them. The politicians must also understand that contrary to the inputs adroitly provided by the bureaucrats in the Ministries of Defence and Finance, it's not really about money any more. It was never a financial issue anyway. In 1947, it was the Prime Minister who attended the funeral of Brig Mohammad Usman, saviour of Jhanjar/Naushera. Decades down the line, funeral of the great military leader Field Marshal Manekshaw was a tame affair with a Minister of State representing the Government of India. No financial implication there; it's just the attitude. It's time the politicians change their attitude and curtail the role of bureaucracy in the so called civilian control over the Military. If anyone needs to be controlled, it's the bureaucrats who are actually undermining national security by running down the Armed Forces. It's time the politicians stood alongside soldiers.

5

Land Border Dynamics on a Progressive Grid (Indian Context)

Dr AP Maheshwari

Border management is an important domain of our National Security, not only from the strategic point of view but from the economic too. Which is, right from keeping a strict vigil on the anti-national elements, the terror module, smugglers, drug peddlers and human traffickers to moving on to the problem of refugees and illegal migration, that too amidst varied terrains changing contours from time to time. A combination of tactics need to be used in varying degrees to evolve an equilibrium that may sustain in a multi-agency, multi-mode environment. Balancing various vectors is indeed a challenging task. Moreover, through the digital world and social media, the operatives no longer need to cross the border. They can brainwash the people within and mutate through them. With various subcultural dissonances between

---

Note: Views expressed in this article by Dr AP Maheshwari are personal.

various agencies that have developed over a period of time, and given the lack of effective coordination mechanism as well as a non-cohesive data base, the synergetic outcome is persistently sub-optimal. The 'silos' culture hampers the desirable governance of the borders. Maintaining friendly borders with countries like Bangladesh, the Indian agencies may now be required to change their modus operandi. The demographic commonality, socio-cultural semblance, a need for economic synergy along with security issues, a need for cooperation during crises situations – all together call for a shift from the restrictive mode to that of the facilitating mode. Illegal trade causes a huge loss to the economy. The present condition of 'opportunity loss' has to be converted into a win-win situation through well managed land posts between the countries. While the integrated check posts facilitate the win-win situation, the collaborative format inter-se all the agencies needs to be evolved as intrinsically as we have succeeded in evolving at the airports. Even across the land border, the security agencies need to think in terms of common data base and joint security drills. Economic synergy between the nations should be given due priority without compromising their security. For this the security based on numerical strength of the soldiers has to be replaced with advanced technologically integrated systems. Technological foot prints may provide a better as well as an undisputable control. The drive towards non lethality also calls for effective remote surveillance and timely intervention by dedicated teams that are well trained for the job. There is no doubt that oscillation in political environment may create neo-conflicts from time to time, however, the economic as well as cultural interests do act as the leverage factors.

The trends across the globe indicate that participation of civic society in border management dynamics is increasingly becoming important. Strategically, direct war is being substituted by proxy war, which hovers around the civic society. Economic synergy too calls for well managed ICPs in a mutually collaborative environment. Migration issues, multi-purpose national identity cards, work permits, refugee status and such similar domains can be better handled with the increasing participation of the civic society close to the borders. We then need to optimize the mutual interests of the concerned various stakeholders. Economic, cultural and security forums find their ways to open dialogues and attain higher synergy levels. International norms and legalities too get operationalized through such participative environment. The right impetus to the work culture further enthuses positive perceptions that dissolves all cognitive barriers.

The switch over from a restrictive environment to a facilitating mode is not so easy. It needs to be done very intelligently and with gradual adaptation. Pakistan and Bangladesh borders provide a glimpse of various contrasts that we have discussed here-in-before. The Nepal and China borders are also witnessing various changes emanating from proxy control of civic population, economic and cultural dominance through unobtrusive tactics over a period of time. There may not be any direct war, but changing the equations within the civic society through the manipulations of socio-cultural and economic vectors, leads to the desired impact.

The intelligence inputs of such a game are entirely different from the security warnings at the micro and semi-macro level. In other words, many such inputs get lost as forces at the cutting edge level are not tuned to scan them successfully. The 'silos' effect further prohibits intelligent collaboration of numerically spread uniformed soldiers and not so visible operatives of customs, immigration, enforcement directorate, narcotic control bureau or other such agencies. In context of the border, many still fail to differentiate between 'border security' and 'border management'. Hence, a case for collaborative work culture between various agencies, participation of civic society, facilitating border management for better synergies appear to be the key factors in those times to come.

Now, there is an emerging thought process whether we need these borders at all. Can there be borderless integrations where people speak of 'Roti Beti Ka Rishta'. Can't there be smart cities across the borders providing for facilitating access on either side. Providing land and water route through the country can bring economic costs to a low. Bangladesh has provided such avenues to India for the transportation of goods in the North-East. There can be endless collaborations in the field of telecom, water resources, power generation etc irrespective of fencing on the boundaries.

Amidst various options of control, joint collaborations will provide higher equilibrium options which will generate more win-win situations for both the countries. Whereas data sharing, joint patrolling, digital watch on the borders through integrated intelligent systems may help control prohibited movements, terror modules and illegal migrations, regular trade may generate economic synergy for both the countries with the series of multiplier effects. Lack of a proper approach channelizes the economic margins into the illegal domains that create a parallel economy. However, much depends on the political relationships and mature diplomacy levels. Any sono-cultural impediments tool have to be mitigated through such handlers and through right perception management.

Since such an approach hovers much beyond the fencing on the border or linear policing alongside the fence, there is also a case for making the federal governments partners in the foreign policy issues so as to facilitate various activities where role of federal State and the local population are crucial for the sustainability of such progressive options.

Theoretically, it seems relevant as well as feasible to go in for such options, but its implementation to the point of optimality may see many oscillations. Quite some waters would have flown below the bridge before the systems mature. Actually, there may even be adverse impacts in the short run. There may also be trade-offs. One needs to tread carefully between the BOPs – ie Balance of Power vs Balance of Payment.

6

Justice Delayed is Justice Denied

Dr PK Agrawal

WHAT IS JUSTICE?

End of law is justice. Society exists because justice is there. Justice ensures balance between two rival claims. It helps in social engineering. It brings equilibrium in the society. Justice is also referred to as 'Dharma'. Salmond defines law as body of principles recognized and applied by the State in the administration of justice. Thus the law made by the legislatures and rules, notifications, regulations, etc, made and implemented by the executive branch of the State form part of law and should aim at delivery of justice. Delay in delivery of judgments, orders or decisions, has caused havoc by denying rights of people and hence denied them justice.

In countries like India, people wait for years for judgments or orders by the courts or tribunals or quasi-judicial bodies. When these judgments or orders are not received after long wait, they get frustrated and lose faith in the judiciary and executive and many of them take law in their own hands and violence erupts in the society. Thus, the purpose of law is defeated ie to maintain equilibrium and peace in the society. Judicial Reform is one of the instruments to tackle the problem of delayed justice.

If the stream of justice is denied up, there will be discontent, upheaval and explosion in the society. The judicial system works as a safety valve in the society. The purpose of judicial reform is to build a credible justice system that will provide agency/channel for citizens to secure their rights through legitimate process. The State is accountable to them.

The citizens should be enabled to resolve their mutual disputes in a free, fair and speedy manner including disputes against the mighty government. Speedy disposal of cases is said to be a component of personal liberty.[1]

PROBLEM OF DELAY

This problem of delay in delivery of justice has been catching attention for many decades. Union Government brought about comprehensive amendments in procedural civil law ie Code of Civil Procedure in the year 1999 and in 2002 but the same have not proved to be efficacious remedy. The court on some ground or the other keep on denying the rights of speedy justice to the citizens of India on grounds of grammatical/ literal interpretation of the law of procedure and inherent power of the court to deliver justice.[2]

However, courts alone are not to be blamed. Even the substantive laws made by the legislatures provide lot of scope for delay. Thirdly, the executive, or quasi-judicial bodies like revenue courts or administrative tribunals indulge into the same type of delaying tactics. One fails to understand in India whether compliance with the procedure or delivery of justice is goal of the courts or quasi-judicial tribunals.

REASONS OF DELAY

As per government reports,[3] by 31st March 2014, about 2.74 crore cases were pending in the District and Subordinate Courts with the rate of constant increase of pendency about 1.94% whereas cases pending in all High Courts were 44.8 lakh with the rate of increase of 0.51%. The Supreme Court is the only court in India which has the minimum pendency of 65,970 cases as on 30.06.2016. The Supreme Court has disposal of cases more than the filing of cases. This is the golden formula to tackle pendency of cases in courts. Other courts and tribunals account for total pendency of about 1.5 crore or more cases. The cases in High Courts and District Courts are pending for about five years on an average. The increase in pendency of cases is due to various reasons such as population explosion, industrial and commercial development, emergence of socio-economic measures touching the life of the citizens at all levels, lawyers strikes, multilayer litigations, etc and increased institution of cases on account of awareness of the rights on the part of citizens.

The Supreme Court has shown the way. The steep decrease in pendency of cases in the Supreme Court is due to their concerted steps taking viz fixing of cases and their allocation to benches through computer network, grouping and classification of cases involving similar question of laws, setting up of specialized benches, computerization of records, etc.

MEASURES UNDERTAKEN TO CURTAIL DELAYS

The problem of delay has been addressed by the judiciary and the government from time to time. Rankin Committee (1924), Arrears Committee (1949), Law Commission's 14th Report (1958), Review Committee, Government of India (1967), Arrears Committee (1972), Jagdish Chandra Committee (1986), Law Commission's reports viz 77th, 79th, 97th, 99th and 124th, Malimath Committee (1989-90), Law Ministers Conference (1992), 154th Report of the Law Commission on CrPC (1996), 156th Report of the Law Commission on the Indian Panel Code (1997), Shetty Commission's Report (1999), Amendments in the CPC in years 1999 and 2002, and recommendations of the National Commission to Review the Working of the Constitution (2002) deliberated the subject extensively and arrived at various suggestions.[4] These suggestions can be summed up under five groups.

Judge Strength and Appointment of Judges

According to the Chief Justice of India the Judge strength is the single most solution to tackle delay in disposal of cases. He made an emotional plea and wondered during the Chief Ministers and Chief Justice conference in the presence of Prime Minister of India in April 2016 why it is not being done at the rate of 50 judges per million population which has been recommended by various commissions and even by the Department-related Parliamentary Standing Committee on Home Affairs in its 86th Report and it has also been laid down by the Supreme Court in the All India Judges Association case[5] that the Judge strength in India should be achieved at the rate of 50 per million in the next five years. The Union

Government and State Governments accept this in principle without any concrete steps, because it will involve huge expenditure of more than ₹14,000 crore, followed by huge recurring expenditure. Secondly Public Service Commission and High Courts will not be able to recruit so many judges. Simultaneously the Public Works Departments will not be able to construct additional courts and increased number of residences in a time bound manner. There is already a huge unfilled vacancies of judges in District Courts to the tune of 2200 judicial officers and there are vacancies of more than 150 judges in various High Courts in the country. The Supreme Court has struck down the National Judicial Appointments Commission Act, 2014 as regards process of selection and appointment of Judges to the High Courts and the Supreme Court and accountability of judges as threatening the independence of the judiciary as well as separation of power which are basic features of the Constitution of India[6]. Thus, there are differences on collegium system between the Supreme Court and the Union Government and **'Memorandum of Procedure'** is still in limbo. If the strength of judges is increased in next five years, it will be available to tackle the present pendency of cases and subsequent pendency of cases which will definitely multiply in future.

Procedures to be Simplified

To accelerate disposal of cases and remove bottlenecks coming in the way of providing speedy and inexpensive justice, there is need to amend and strictly observe the provisions in the existing procedural laws and regulations ie the High Court Acts and Rules, Civil Procedure Code (CPC), the Criminal Procedure Code, The Indian Evidence Act etc. There should be provision for issuing notices to the defendants/non-applicants at the first hearing itself. Notices should also be issued by courier or speed post or electronic mail. Time limit for arguments be fixed. It will be better if written arguments are encouraged and entertained. The amendment in CPC in 1999 and 2002 may be termed as *magna carta* for the Indian Judicial System. The amendments *inter alia* provide for time limits at various stage of a suit like service of plaint to the defendant within 30 days of institution of suit even through courier, filing of written statement within 30 days extendable up to 90 days, examinations of witnesses through commissioner as per general power of court to extend time up to 30 days, delivery of judgment within 60 days compulsory pre-litigation settlement efforts and restriction of number of adjournments to three to a party in a suit.

But these epoch making legislative amendments have been whittled down by the Apex Court in the case of Salem Advocate Bar Association cases. The Supreme Court held that the amendment is not curtailing the court's power to allow more than three adjournments to a party in a suit. Similarly the court held that the new provision does not specify a time limit within which summons ought to be served to the defendant by the court. The new provisions of 2002 in CPC fixing the time limit of 90 days from the date of service of summons for filing written statement has been relaxed by the Supreme Court interpreting it as merely directory and not mandatory.[7]

Adjournment as Main Cause of Delay

Inspite clear provision in Order XVII, Rule 1, lawyers take adjournments on various grounds *inter alia* the illness of the lawyer or the party to the suit, the advocate's engagement in other courts, non-receipt of required papers and documents from the client, fresh appointment of advocate by the client, a prayer for transfer of the case from one court to another. Sometime, adjournments are granted by the court due to absence of presiding officer from the court either due to he or she being on leave or busy otherwise. As a result, the public is losing faith in the justice delivery system. Whenever they go to the court with the hope of getting an order, they mostly come out with the next date of hearing after paying fees to the advocate.

Interestingly, there are also some clients and advocates whose vested interest is only in delaying the judicial process, especially in matters of huge arrears of taxes, fees and other arrear, and dues to the Government. It can be scientifically observed that when the case file is to be brought to the court, it takes about one hour in taking out the file from the record room, listing it by the assistant concerned and placing it in the court by the court attendant. Thus, the precious time of the court is wasted while granting adjournments. One minute working of the Delhi High Court entailed an average expenditure of ₹14,771 in 2011-2012. With such a great amount of tax payer's money going into working of the courts, the system gains nothing from adjournments.

The legal fraternity overlooks the fact that majority of the clients and *bona fide* litigants come before courts and tribunals with the hope that their petitions/cases/applications will be expeditiously disposed of and will not end up filling up the dockets of courts for years and the lawyer's pocket. Even generations have to wait for orders from the source of justice in the country. Judgments/orders are implemented not because there is enforcement machinery but due to the faith of the people in the judiciary. It is, therefore, hoped that all will work unitedly so that the curse of adjournments on the Indian judiciary is wiped out.

The Supreme Court held[8] that the grant of adjournment by a court has to be on showing special and extraordinary circumstances. It cannot be in routine. While considering the prayer for grant of adjournment, it is necessary to keep in mind the legislative intent to restrict the grant of adjournment. Even in cases which may not strictly come within the category of circumstances beyond the control of a party, the court by resorting to the provision of higher costs which can also include punitive costs in the discretion of the court, adjournment beyond three can be granted having regard to the injustice that may result on refusal thereof, with reference to the peculiar facts of a case.

Thus, the courts and lawyers are still required to attach proper sanctity to provision restricting the adjournments to three to a party of suit. In one criminal case, advocate and former Law Minister of India Kapil Sibbal demanded in the Supreme Court that cost of adjournment should be awarded after deducting from salary of the judges concerned as an extreme steps. The foreign jurisdictions are surprised as to why there is provision of adjournment in the Indian Judicial System.

Court Procedure and Mechanism

Court procedure is very important as regards High Courts and the Supreme Court because these courts have their own rules of procedure and they are not governed by the CPC or CrPC. The Malimath Committee (1989-90) known as Arrears

Committee, has suggested extensive reforms in procedure of the High Court's as follows:

- (i) Abolition of original civil jurisdiction of High Court.
- (ii) Abolition of Letters Patent Appeals.
- (iii) Discouraging multiplicity of appeals, especially from the quasi-judicial tribunals.
- (iv) High Courts to specify category of cases which could be heard by a single Judge or by a Division Bench.
- (v) Convention to be evolved to discourage granting of adjournment.
- (vi) Limitation on presentation of oral arguments, long elaborate judgments.
- (vii) Reserved judgments should be delivered within 90 days.

Many of the High Courts have implemented these recommendations but some are still in the process even after the lapse of twenty five years or more. The Supreme Court presents an ideal system to control arrears except that it gives little leverage to the senior advocates of the court.

In the case of District/Subordinate Courts, the following procedure may be very relevant –

- (a) Court should be well prepared with the facts of the case and relevant law applicable.
- (b) Courts should maintain the punctuality of time and should work for full hours of court and discipline should be maintained for timely disposal of the case.
- (c) Courts should have control over Daily Diary of cases.
- (d) Adjournments should not be granted and heavy costs be imposed for adjournments.

The court is more or less manoeuvred measurements by intelligent or tricky lawyers. It is said in India that justice is what the lawyers dictate. Thus, the lawyers will continue to play an important role in delivery of justice in courts and to expedite the process of disposal of cases. The counsels should also observe their professional duties/ethics in the interest of justice for speedy disposal by taking least possible adjournments and should be well prepared for the case so that time of court is not wasted. They should avoid multifarious applications to delay proceedings.

Service of Summons and Warrants

Provisions have been added in the CPC to fix time limit for most of the processes in the court for which delay is caused. But the Supreme Court does not agree. As regards service of summons, the Apex Court says that the words 'on such day not beyond thirty days from the date of the institution of the suit', do not mean that the summons must be served within thirty days of the date of the institution of the suit. The words added by the amendment, fix outer time frames by providing that steps must be taken within thirty days from the date of the institution of the suit.[9] There is a revolutionary change which strives to involve the plaintiff in service of summons and introduces a new system of service of summons through courier service which was earlier dependent on service of summons which was a very delaying process. If plaintiff is involved at every stage, he would not blame for all the delays because the system and defendants or respondents also contribute to delays.

In criminal matter, there is no other way except to serve warrant through the concerned police station as because the accused will not accept warrant otherwise. The cases in a criminal court should be divided police station-wise and exclusive personal or constables may be earmarked to serve notices, summons or warrants from the courts. Similarly, the superintendent of police or higher officer should constantly monitor service of warrants etc. There should be separation between the investigation and prosecution wing. Due to lack of scientific investigation, the cases are prolonged.

In Russia and some other countries the investigation is completed within 2-3 days after commission of the crime because everybody concerned gathers at the site after commission of crime. Even newly created Fast Track Courts are handicapped to undertake expeditious disposal of cases due to non-service of summons or warrants.

The Court held that a provision for summary dismissal of criminal appeal is not unfair if certain safeguards against arbitrary dismissal are incorporated.[10] The Supreme Court has gone to the extent holding that 'a procedural law is void if it does not provide for speedy trial.[11]

But the Supreme Court becomes soft whenever any Bar Association or Senior Advocate appears before the Hon'ble Court for relief from rigorous or time bound solutions.

Delay in Delivery of Judgments

According to the amendment in CrPC, the judgment should normally be delivered within 60 days after completing hearing of the case. This will also help to ensure transparency and integrity in judicial working. It is generally accepted tradition that the judgment or order is delivered in substance after the conclusion of the hearing but the detailed judgment should not be delayed beyond 60 days.

The party is interested to hear the order and judgment and not long judgments for academic purpose.

Working Hours of Courts

The courts in India are working for less days than the government offices. The Shetty Commission has suggested that vacation of District/Subordinate Courts should be cut by 15 days and the District Court should work for at least 36 hours in a week. The litigant visiting the courts find that after the lunch the courts are not active. If courts hour of working is increased by half an hour, lot of pendency of cases will be tackled. Other alternatives like night courts in the same court buildings have not found favour with the judiciary as well as with the lawyers. This indicates that judiciary itself should play a major role in reduction of arrears through self-restraint.

Systemic Solutions

The cases are so much delayed that sometimes the cases are disposed of after the demise of the petitioners and there is no taker of the judgment of the court. The litigant lose interest and energy in pursuing the cases because they have to pay fat fees to their counsels and have to travel time and again to courts where the Peshkar grants adjournments even without putting the file to the presiding officer by taking a petty bribe from the other party. As a result, either the petitioners tries to compromise with the opposite party or in criminal cases, he takes revenge against the accused person whenever he is on bail or otherwise moves in the society. People get scared when they find that mafia or gangsters or serious offenders roam in open in-spite of several cases pending against them. Thus, the basic purpose of law is defeated. The problem is so acute that it cannot be solved by superficial measures. Legislatures, executive and judiciary have to sit together and work out a feasible solution.

Some of the systemic solutions suggested are as follows:

Alternative Dispute Resolution (ADR)

Section 89 of the Civil Procedure Code provides for compulsory pre-litigative settlement. The dispute before the court will be referred for conciliation or settlement by way of mediation, conciliation or arbitration through Lok Adalat or otherwise through the court appointed mediator. According to the Supreme Court, 90% of the cases are settled out of court in certain countries where ADR has been successful. The modalities have since under the title "Civil Procedure-Alternative Dispute Resolution and Mediation Rules, 2003" been formulated by the Committee appointed by the Supreme Court and it is expected that implementation of Section 89 will revolutionize the judicial system and tribunals or quasi-judicial fora. At the same time, the free legal aid will be available with the proper implementation of the Legal Services Authorities Act, 1987. Similarly, the Committee has drafted the Model High Court Rules, 2003 for Model Case Flow Management Rules. It is hoped that these two rules will help in a big way to tackle delay and pendency at District and Subordinate Courts and at High Courts.

Professional Improvement

There can be no choice for outside reforms or control by some other organ of the State. The Chief Justice of India after meeting with the Chief Justices of High Courts has adopted a 'Code of Ethics of the Judges – 1997'. It requires to be implemental in all respects. There are lot of complaints of corruption in District and Subordinate judiciary. The High Courts have well laid down vigilance mechanism but its functioning requires lot of gearing up in view of growing cases of corruption at lower levels. Some mechanism has to be devised at the district level or the lower judiciary should be subjected to vigilance by the normal vigilance set up of the State Government. To that extent, the Judges (Protection) Act, 1985 can be amended to instill faith in the judiciary of the common people. The judiciary as an institution works in cooperation with lawyers and they are officers of the Court. Therefore, without improvement of legal profession, there will not be substantial improvement in performance of courts as courts heavily depend or submissions by both sides of lawyers. The legal profession was unorganized so far. Anybody could practice in Court, or Tribunals after obtaining LLB degree and registering with any Bar Council. It has produced a large number of briefless lawyers who cannot meet their both ends. On the other hand, there is gradual creation of neo-capitalists among lawyers. Curtailment of adjournment can have more job for unemployed lawyers. Now the Bar Council of India has made stiff rules before one can be inducted in practice. Secondly, number of high level professional colleges like national law schools have been opened which have given a new look to one of the oldest and most popular profession. However, still lawyers' strike now and then on trivial issues add to the delay in disposal of cases. In the western Uttar Pradesh, lawyers have been on strike for a long time on the demand of opening of bench of High Court of Allahabad in the western Uttar Pradesh. Without a competent and sincere legal profession, speedy disposal of cases will be a day dream.

Infrastructural Facilities for Judiciary

The First National Judicial Pay Commission has provided lot of better salaries, perquisites and facilities to Judges and Magistrates of the District Courts which are even better then the top Indian Administrative Service in the country. Governments have provided lot of funds for construction of court-building and residences for judges under the Centrally Sponsored Scheme and for computerization of courts. As a result, there is lot of improvement in infrastructure of courts. However if judges strength has to be increased to 50 per million, this infrastructure will be inadequate and buildings cannot be built in a year. Therefore, the judiciary has to act fast to liquidate pending cases without waiting for the infrastructural facilities in place. Cases are pending not just due to shortage of judges. It is shown that the ratio per million of population is less in Punjab and Tamil Nadu as compared to other States, yet their rate of disposal of cases is higher than other States.[12]

However, there is lot of improvement in case filing, case fixing, publishing of cause list, placement of daily orders on Internet and website etc. Times are not far off when everything will be computerized and the courts in India will be E-Courts. However, it is still doubtful whether a litigant from village will be able to take advantage of it immediately. However, to a large extent, he has been relieved of exploitation of their counsel as regards fixing of cases and orders on various dates. Litigants can also get copy of judgment from the Internet. In the Supreme Court and in all High Courts, facilitation/Enquiry Centres, have been set up where the public can know the status of the cases on Internet and on voice mail. These should be more financial autonomy to the courts so that they have not to look up to government for every small thing for example, the judges are required to be trained and retrained to keep abreast with the latest judicial pronouncements of the Supreme Court and High Courts. The training institutions require lot of funds for their day to day running and maintenance. The National Commission to review the working of the Constitution has recommended that there is concurrent obligation on the Union Government to meet the expenditure for subordinate courts. Therefore, sufficient funds from national resources be allocated to meet the demands of the State Judiciary in each of the States.

Governments Role

The State Governments and the Union Government should earmark adequate funds according to increasing requirement of judiciary. That will give them good return also as their taxes involved in cases will be recovered. They should also ensure that Administrative Tribunals, Income Tax Appellate Tribunal, Rent Control Tribunal, Family Courts, Labour Tribunals, Debt Recovery Tribunal, Competition Commission of India, Consumer Redressal Fora at district, State and national levels and Fast Track Courts etc, are duly looked after and their performance is duly monitored administratively as well. These quasi-judicial authorities are taking lot of burden of the regular courts successfully. However, these are also gradually going into the shoes and vicious circle of procedure like the regular courts as their presiding officers are senior judges who bring good and bad experience as judges with them and are quite conservative with changing times of information technology.

The Governments at the State and Union should also see that obsolete and outdated laws are scrapped and substantive laws are made to keep pace with the changing times. Last but not the least, the quality of legislative drafting should be such as it leaves minimum loopholes in statutes and give least scope for manoeuvring by courts or intelligent lawyers to avoid laws. Proper drafting of laws can help to eliminate delays and multiplicity of litigation.

The government officers responsible for non submissions or delayed submission or vague and evasive replies should be personally fixed and costs should be recovered from them. This will reduce lot of unnecessary litigation arising from the side of government.[13] Who is the major litigant.

Setting-up of Nyaya Panchayats or Gram Nyayalayas

Gram Nyayalayas when set up and operated would be informal and not strictly technical. The expenditure of poor litigants will be reduced to a minimum and it would take justice at the door steps of litigants. Earlier the Nyaya Panchayats set up in Uttar Pradesh and other States in 1950s and 1960s, disposed off crores of cases. The Law Commission in its 154th Report has suggested to adopt the Andhra Pradesh Mandal Nyayalaya Act. The Gramin Nyayalayas Act, 2008 has created about 5,000 Gramin Nyayalayas in India. "The effective functioning of Nyaya Panchayats can facilitate the speedy settlement of many disputes at the village level itself. They provide for the speedy and summary disposal of cases. Structurally the system has the advantage of easy and accessibility speedy settlement of disputes, openness etc. But enough steps should be designed to protect these institutions from the influence of rural rich and vested interests.[14]

CONCLUSIONS

In so many judgments, the Supreme Court has re-invented the speedy disposal of cases as one of the fundamental rights under Article 21 of the Constitution of India. All courts in India are to observe this fundamental right though the rules of procedure are the handmaid of justice but not its mistress. The Supreme Court has coined the term "judicial impact assessment" as is practised in the United States. It will cover the budgetary requirement from the government, review of performance of the statute to achieve its objectives and speedy dispensation of justice by the courts from the lowest level to the highest one. In the matter of denial of speedy justice, the Court expressed the concern at delay in disposal of cases. The concerned authorities were directed to do needful in the matter urgently before situation goes totally out of control.[15] It is hoped that the courts will invoke their inherent power to make available justice to the public at their doorsteps with minimum expenditure and with minimum efforts by the petitioner. The courts can further be strengthened in their mission by expeditious services of notices of courts, adequate training of judges, improvement in legal profession and legal education by way of necessary amendments in substantive and procedural laws and setting up Gramin Nyayalayas in India.

If required, Union Government will further bring amendments in Code of Civil Procedure in keeping with observations of the Supreme Court in its various judgments. In any case, the people should not be denied justice because of delay in disposal of cases in courts or quasi-judicial tribunals.

REFERENCES

1. Raj Deo Sharma *vs* State of Bihar (1999), 7 SCC 507.
2. Salem Advocate Bar Association TN *vs* Union of India (2005), 6 SCC 344.
3. *Court News*, April-June 2014, Supreme Court Website.
4. Agrawal, Dr PK, 'Concrete Approach to Judicial Reform', Working Paper No 2-7, Rajiv Gandhi Institute for Contemporary Studies, New Delhi, p 36.
5. All India Judges Association (3) *vs* Union of India (2002), 4 SCC 24.
6. Supreme Court Advocate-on-Records Bar Association *vs* Union of India, judgment on December, 16, 2015.
7. Kailash *vs* Nanhku, AIR 2005 SC 2441.
8. Ibid 2, p 354.
9. Salem Advocate Bar Association, Tamil Nadu *vs* Union of India, AIR 2003 Supreme Court, 189, p 189.
10. Sita Ram *vs* State of Uttar Pradesh, AIR 1983 SC 65.
11. Sher Singh *vs* State of Punjab (1983), 2 SCC 344.
12. *The Times of India*, 11th October 2016, Editor: Anshul Chaturvedi, Bennet Coleman & Co Ltd, New Delhi.
13. Ibid 2, p 346.
14. Chaturvedi, Archana, *Judiciary, Government and Politics*, 2014, Arpan Publications, New Delhi, p 312.
15. Moses Wilson *vs* Katuriba, AIR 2008 SC 379.

7

Urban Terrorism and the Lone-Wolf: Intrinsic Limitations of the Indian Nation-State in Response

Dr NC Asthana

INTRODUCTION

Amongst the countries affected by terrorism, India is in a unique and particularly vulnerable position. Given the vast size of the country and a society replete with all sorts of diversities, discordant notes and fissiparous tendencies, India lends itself eminently to acts of terrorism. Unfortunately, we cannot afford to blindly ape the Western models of dealing with terrorism. The response of the State to such acts is confounded by the fact that they could be committed by small groups and lone-wolves that are difficult to be tracked, traced and punished by the process of law. The acts of terror in the West are committed largely by people from outside; the acts of terrorism in India have a significant component of indigenous

Note: Views expressed in this article by Dr NC Asthana are personal.

elements amongst the perpetrators. This means that every State action must be taken with great care and prudence; otherwise, it runs the risk of the possibility of a gullible and susceptible section of the population accusing the State of selective persecution and violation of human rights, thereby setting up a vicious cycle of recruitment and prosecution. The 'persecution complex' may force them to identify their real or perceived grievances with trans-national issues and forces – this is what explains the joining of the ISIS (or at least sympathizing with it over the Net) by so many Indians from across the country.

THE DISTINCTION BETWEEN INSURGENCIES AND TERRORISM

An insurgency can be defined as a struggle between a non-ruling group (non-State actors) and the ruling authorities (State actors) in which the former consciously employs political resources (organizational skills, propaganda and/or demonstrations) and instruments of (ostensibly illegal) violence to gain political concessions or outright independence from the existing system. Terrorism might also have its origin in issues or grievances similar to those that lead to insurgencies but they are not essential conditions. Terrorism could be resorted to for very 'limited objectives' too. Insurgents may or may not employ terrorism as a tool in their efforts. The four stages in the classical progression of insurgency are: organization or subversive stage; terrorism stage; guerrilla warfare stage; and mobile warfare stage. In practice, insurgencies may often be obliged to fall back to the terrorism stage whenever the government response becomes effective. Many insurgencies may never even get past this stage. **However, in a modern society, it is relatively easy to maintain a certain level of terrorism and thus to continue the terrorism stage almost indefinitely**. The LTTE which had progressed almost to the mobile warfare stage frequently fell back to the terrorism phase. Insurgencies necessarily require the participation of a large number of people in it; terrorists can go about their business with a group of just a few people. In fact even the reasons for terrorism may not relate to any large section of the population.

TERRORISM'S IMPACTS MUCH BIGGER THAN ITS REAL STRENGTH

The methods which a terrorist can adopt are limited only by his imagination and as such are not of any great consequence. What is of consequence is the impact of his actions. The impact of a terrorist act is both physical and psychological, the latter being more important. The physical element is impermanent or may be even immaterial. When a bomb explodes, there may not be any significant damage. **However, the psychological impact is always there and its overall effect may be greater than that of the physical impact**. Even if a bomb does not result in many casualties or extensive damage to property, the very fact that a bomb could be planted at a certain place goes on to show that the terrorists could breach the security of the State and thus the act damages the credibility of the State. A terrorist strike is therefore necessarily intended to create worry, fear, or panic in the minds of the target. Terrorism derives its strength almost entirely from the psychological impact of his strikes on the government through the reactions amongst the people and most importantly, in the media.

OPERATIONAL ADVANTAGES OF TERRORISM VIS-A-VIS INSURGENCIES

In terms of efficiency, a terrorist movement is much more efficient than an insurgency. Collecting the means of committing acts of terrorism is no problem at all – even individuals can do that and that too legitimately from e-commerce, without ever stepping out of their houses. Remote control RF switches with a range of about 2 miles for activating IEDs are available for as low as $7; infrared switches are available for $15. With a staggering 1.89 million tons of emulsion explosive produced in the country for legitimate commercial activities and where it is rather easy for criminals to 'divert' (not pilfer) some explosive from genuine users, which terrorist would look for RDX from abroad? One who allows the figure of 1.89 billion kilos manufactured by 73 licensed factories (second only to the USA in the whole world) sink in his mind will understand and appreciate that any hope of the police to keep track of the explosives, particularly after it is delivered to the licensed users, is simply impossible.

The perpetrators are so very few and their potential targets so immensely large in number that in practice there is little that the governments can do to contain them. It is impossible to protect the myriads of targets that any modern society presents. Insurgencies, because they take upon themselves a grand objective and cumbersome means, have a much higher chance of failure than terrorists. One of the great strengths of terrorists is that they take small tasks and small objectives upon themselves. The selection of targets is only a matter of convenience.

WHY INSURGENCIES ARE LIKELY TO LOSE IN THE END?

Insurgencies, by definition, have to be mass movements. This means that the insurgents are obliged to rally the support of a large number of people. This means that the chances of some betrayal or infiltration are greatly increased. Since the standard police approach depends on informers, it is easier to deal with insurgencies. In any case, in this era, agitating the people is a much harder task than what romantic revolutionaries believe, particularly in those nations where consumerism has taken control of the collective psyche of the people and people are naturally reluctant to disturb the *status quo* in anything.

The terrorist, on the other hand, need not bother about agitating the population for he is not really or critically dependent upon them. The terrorists may therefore go about their work without involving the people at large. There may be sections of population that render some secret logistic help to them; there may be sections which are silent admirers; but terrorists may exist and thrive even if such sections do not exist. Majority of the people of this country do not have any idea of the political or ideological content of any insurgent movement, and for good reason. Since the people are not bothered, the media is not bothered either – in the end, insurgencies (and that too in some fringe, deep or forested area of the country) fail to build up any real pressure on the Government. **Terrorism hogs headlines and builds up instant pressure**.

Terrorists fight the 'ideal asymmetric war' because they refuse to fight the government on its terms. The insurgents who try to take on the might of the establishment on their terms are bound to lose.

WHY WESTERN MODELS OF WAR ON TERROR WOULD NOT WORK IN INDIA?

Western 'War on Terror': Hype versus Reality

The Indian media cries that we must replicate the Western models of fighting terror here too. Examples are cited of the strict laws enacted in the Western world. The USA Patriot Act of 2001 (Uniting and Strengthening America by Providing Appropriate Tools Required to Intercept and Obstruct Terrorism Act of 2001), for example, has allowed the US security agencies to search telephone, e-mail communications, medical, financial and other records and eased restrictions on foreign intelligence gathering within the United States. Countries like Australia have given "stop and search" powers to their police, which allow the police to stop and search people. The country also has a "Control Order", that allows the police to approach a closed court and ask for restrictions to be placed on someone who poses a terror threat. The restrictions can limit who the suspect can talk to, where the person can go and what devices the suspect can use (phone and Internet). The UK's Counter-Terrorism Act 2008 and Counter Terrorism and Security Act 2015 provide for grossly increased police powers.

As the recent spate of terrorist attacks in the USA amply shows, the tremendous hype notwithstanding, the anti-terror laws of the USA have not produced commensurate results.

There were as many as **7 terrorist attacks in the USA in 2015 and 11 in 2016 till September 19**. (http://www.johnstonsarchive.net/terrorism/wrjp255a.html)

American Approach

In respect of acts of terrorism on US soil, the Americans are obsessed with terrorism by Muslims, the ISIS and the Taliban, etc. In States supported by the USA such as Afghanistan, the current US doctrine regards the insurgents or terrorists as outsiders (or at least 'trouble makers with a foreign ideology') by the native population in a fixed geographic region. The current US doctrine is based on the concept of "fight, secure, build". The old WHAM (winning hearts and minds) is now being peddled by the Americans as 'decency and brotherhood' approach. At the operational level, however, critics maintain, it translates into: "Try to be nice, but if they don't go along with the programme 'manipulate' them. If that doesn't work, kill them." That it has not worked even in Afghanistan is evident from the fact that in spite of the US having spent a whopping $ 685.6 billion on the war effort and having pumped the latest technology in the war, the Taliban remain undefeated and President Ashraf Ghani had recently (September 2016) been obliged to sign a Peace Deal with the warlord Gulbuddin Hekmatyar, the notorious 'Butcher of Kabul'.

Israeli Approach

The Israeli approach has been described as 'stabilization operations' in a prolonged low-intensity conflict zone with a special focus on people of their own ethnic origin. As a long term measure, realizing that reconciliation is not really possible, their traditional technique has been physical segregation of the target populace. The Americans also copied it in Iraq where vast areas have been sealed off behind concrete walls and sand berms, creating what they call 'gated communities'. Over-watch is maintained increasingly through unmanned aerial platforms – described as 'aerial occupation'. At operational level they place great emphasis on actionable intelligence at company level. The Israelis have frequently been criticized on the ground of '**overkill**'.

Since their tactical gains have often mesmerized uninitiated observers, it merits a critical evaluation. The basis of the Israeli approach of 'overkill' is an unstated belief that a 'proportionate response' is not an effective deterrent to terrorism. Scott Atran, a veteran analyst, argues that "**repeated suicide actions show that massive counterforce alone does not diminish the frequency or intensity of suicide attacks**." Even Richard Boucher, then State Department spokesperson under the hawkish Bush administration doubted the value of Israel's offensive moves, namely, targeted killings, when he stated in July 2001 that "**Israel needs to understand that targeted killings of Palestinians don't end the violence, but are only inflaming an already volatile situation and making it much harder to restore calm**." Daniel Byman has shown in his work *A High Price: The Triumphs and Failures of Israeli Counterterrorism*, that tactical victories eventually become strategic defeats. The killing of Hamas's master bomb-maker, Yahya 'the Engineer' Ayyash, in 1996, for example, no doubt dented Hamas's capabilities for some time, but it also led to a renewed wave of bus bombings. The continuous killing of terrorists in West Bank and Gaza has only led to being more and more of them being produced – in fact Israeli action in those areas has, to a considerable extent, become the global rallying point for susceptible Muslims to take up arms against the so-called Zionist oppression supported by the West, thereby making the West almost an unintended target.

WHY URBAN TERRORISM MAKES SENSE FOR TERRORISTS TARGETING INDIA

Urban terrorism is the most effective tool which terrorists may employ against a State like India. **Given the way the media behaves with all its upper-middle class biases, even a firecracker blast in a posh market of Delhi creates a terrible noise across the country**. Similar examples are found in other countries also. A major strike somewhere deep in Waziristan goes unnoticed whereas even a failed bomb blast in front of a hotel in Islamabad where foreigners stay, attracts attention of the world media. In most of the countries, the interests of the ruling class are aligned with the urban upper or upper-middle classes. Thus urban terrorist strikes produce impacts far greater on them than that by similar strikes in rural areas. **Hence for a terrorist who understand the psyche of a nation, its people, its media and its ruling class, urban terrorism makes eminent sense**. The returns of urban terrorism are certainly disproportionately higher than its innate worth. Its strength lies in two words: anytime and anywhere. The fear that they can strike you anytime and anywhere makes them larger than life. The secret of the power of urban terrorism lies in the fact that they are able to create a climate of fear, panic, disorientation and capitulation out of all proportion to their actual strength courtesy an irresponsible media and an effete population under its influence.

THE STRATEGY AND TACTICS OF THE URBAN TERRORIST

Attacking the Soft Underbelly of the State

The first thing an urban terrorist does is to abandon any pretence to heroism, popular support, or fair play. Urban terrorism is for the cold, calculating, ruthless men who do not mind if they are called cowards. To him, only the impact of his strikes matters. They strike at the softest targets; if they have to make a selection they make it according to the psychological impact it would produce and not by the considerations of the material damage caused. An urban terrorist does not make any effort to change the views or perception of the masses or bring them over to his side. He is the ultimate predator who attacks only the soft underbelly of his target however large or powerful it be. He plays upon the weaknesses of the target people. He brings their hidden fears to the fore. The upper-middle and the upper classes fear nothing more than any damage to their privileged positions and possessions. Urban terrorism threatens them right there. Shopping may no longer be enjoyable because a bomb could explode in the market. Somebody may start shooting at a hotel or crash a car bomb; somebody may fire at some party. Worse, political instability may result as a result of the brouhaha and the stock market may plunge. In short, urban terrorism threatens the very vitals of their happy and cocooned existence.

Hit and Disappear

The urban terrorist is a die-hard realist. He knows that defeating the resources of a large nation-State through guns or bombs would be impossible. On the other hand, they also realize that given the fundamentally flawed approach of the security establishment they are not likely to be faced with the prospect of immediate extinction either. Hence he makes the best of the situation available. He measures his success in terms of how effective he is in creating havoc, a general feeling of insecurity and a loss of confidence in the government besides taxing the resources of the government in chasing shadows. Urban strikes are perfectly suited for a terrorist organization which is low on resources. Fewer men are required; they can conceal themselves easily in an urban environment and there is little which the police can do to secure the myriads of targets which an urban area presents even if they deploy very heavily. It is infinitely easier for the urban terrorist to hit and simply disappear in an urban area. The urban terrorist approach does not require an extensive political apparatus either; rather, closely knit cells do the job.

Disproportionate Impact

Even small urban strikes lead to a great deal of:

- Noise in the media and thus impart a larger-than-life image to the terrorists;
- Panic amongst the urban population which is not used to such acts; once again helping their image;
- Consequent effect on the governments because the urban-centric media and the urban population are key opinion-builders;
- Knee-jerk reactions from the governments and possibly wasteful decisions;
- Perfectly useless diversion of police manpower and resources to urban areas which, in any case, fails to add to their security; and

- The resulting depletion in the other areas which increases their vulnerability even more

India is a particularly vulnerable target in this regard. The media here is habitually given to making more noise than anywhere else in the world for the smallest thing.

LONE-WOLF TERRORIST

By definition, a lone-wolf terrorist is someone who prepares and commits violent acts alone, outside of any command structure and without material assistance from any group. However, he or she may be influenced or motivated by the ideology and beliefs of an external group, and may act in support of such a group.

Intrinsic Advantages of a Lone-Wolf

The lone-wolf terrorist does not lend himself to the usual police methods of crime prevention and investigation. First, he shall not be conspicuous. For all you know, he might be the typical guy living next door. And please note that if he has got even a modicum of brains, he would not sport a beard on a haggard-looking face; wear black shalwar-kameez with a backpack slung over his shoulders, and would not come out of the rented house with always a riding helmet on his head so that his face is not seen, would not make it a point to always go out early and come back late in the night without ever exchanging pleasantries with the neighbours. The secret of the success of the lone-wolf lies in remaining as inconspicuous as possible. He must merge with his surroundings and be one of the 'regular guys'. Unless he was to mount a suicide operation, he will continue living as before and will not necessarily try to sneak out after the strike. Immediate sneaking out arouses suspicion. If he has to leave, he shall leave with a proper excuse to leave. Second, he may not have a police record. Even if he is caught somewhere on some other ground, the total absence of a police record and fingerprint records etc, would ensure his past can never be traced or analysed. Third, and most importantly, by not having many accomplices or no accomplice at all, he ensures that the chances of infiltration or compromise by someone are greatly reduced. The greater the number of persons involved in a project, the higher the chances of inadvertent leakage, some mistake by someone somewhere or infiltration by the police or intelligence agencies – one cannot possible have a large number of members who are all equally dedicated, incorruptible, careful and methodical. Conversely, even if there is a leakage of information from a small group, it is always possible to apply a logical process of successive elimination and figure out who could have been the source of the leak.

Timothy McVeigh's Mistakes are not Likely to be Repeated

Timothy McVeigh, the Oklahoma bomber (one who killed 168 people and injured 680 in a truck-bomb attack on the Alfred P Murrah Federal Building in 1995) had committed three fundamental mistakes that led to his arrest and execution. But for those, he would have got away. **A smarter terrorist would never commit those mistakes and that's what a nation like ours must prepare for**. He had hired a Ryder truck for planting the explosives. That was fine. He expected that when the truck blows up, it will erase all possible signs of identification. But that was not to be. By tracing the Vehicle Identification Number (VIN) on a rear axle found in the wreckage, the FBI identified the vehicle as a Ryder Rental box truck rented from Junction City, Kansas. An intelligent terrorist would have filed off the VIN from all locations. Workers at the rental agency assisted an FBI artist in creating a sketch of the renter, who had used the alias 'Robert Kling'. The sketch was shown in the area. The manager of a local motel identified the sketch as that of a person who had stayed there. Shortly after the bombing, while driving out of the city, McVeigh was stopped by an Oklahoma State Trooper. McVeigh's car had no license plate. That was a terrible mistake – the second. Not only that, McVeigh admitted to the police officer (who noticed a bulge under his jacket) that he had a gun. McVeigh was arrested for driving without licence plate and possession of an illegal firearm because his concealed weapon permit was not legal in Oklahoma. That was the third mistake – an intelligent terrorist would have known the local laws better. Three days later, while still in custody, McVeigh was identified as the subject of the nationwide manhunt.

STRATEGIC CONSEQUENCES OF THE STRIKES OF SMALL GROUPS OR LONE-WOLVES

Two-and-a-Half Front War

The effect of the strikes of terrorists would be felt all the more acutely during times of crisis such as a war or an impending war -- whether it is a single front war with Pakistan or China; or a two-front war with both. The term 'two-and-a-half front war' has been given to a hypothetical situation in which India might have to engage both Pakistan and China simultaneously besides conducting a serious counterinsurgency or counter-terrorist campaign inside. If the insurgents or terrorists launch a systematic campaign of **fifth-columnist action** by way of disrupting communications and attacking Indian army logistics, it would present a very difficult situation.

If they know their job, they would employ their energy and resources in **sabotaging** the lines of communication (such as bridges, roads, railroads, etc) and not waste time in attacking security forces (except may be, attacks on convoys). Steel bridges in particular are rather easy to destroy by explosives – concrete bridges in comparison are somewhat difficult. The elementary techniques to destroy bridges and other structures are very much available in public domain and terrorists do not need any special ISI course for that. And for all you know, the Pakistanis could indeed infiltrate especially trained saboteurs. If the terrorists or saboteurs know their business, the army's supply lines can be easily cut to the utter detriment of any campaign.

Other all-time favourite targets of sabotage (even in hinterland) are power substations; transformers; high voltage pylons (they would not bother to attack power stations, as they have security anyway); derailing rolling stock (particularly those connected with army efforts); passenger trains to spread panic; steel bridges; fuel dumps; runways; grain godowns; mobile switching centres; and spreading rumours of biological/radiological and chemical warfare. They may not have a direct effect on the operations of the armed forces but they have great effect on the general public and thus serve to spread panic.

State's Limitations in Dealing with Terrorist Strikes

Modern society presents a million targets which the fifth-columnists can attack and which will directly or indirectly have an effect on the operations of the armed forces. And they do not really require a sympathetic population, even as it could help. Sabotage can be carried out by small groups. **Being the large country that we are, we have so many assets to protect that even if we close down every single police station and pull out every single paramilitary man from internal security duties, even then we would find it nearly impossible to protect all of them**.

HOW A MATURE NATION MUST RESPOND TO ACTS OF TERRORISM?

Terrorism becomes effective only if the target makes it so. Terrorism, to be successful, expects that the target must respond in a certain manner. The fact of responding in an expected manner is such that it weakens the target, both in image and reality. When a nation responds to a few small blasts as if a national calamity has struck; it unknowingly adorns the culprits with an aura which they don't deserve. **A nation is defeated by the fear and not the fire of terrorists**.

Deny the terrorist the pleasure of the expected response and you have beaten him. One should always keep in mind that while the root causes of terrorism could be political, sociological or whatever, the impact of terrorism is determined to a great extent by the target's behaviour, which is largely psychological in character. The design of the terrorist is to manipulate the target's psychological perceptions to induce it to act in the way it is predisposed to act.

The effort of those who have to combat terrorism must be to refuse to act in a predictable or expected manner, and least of all in a manner that serves the purpose of the terrorists.

Prudent targets must not behave as automatons. For example, if the terrorists perceive a target as powerful and self-righteous, they should expect it to over-react; certainly they would not expect it to suffer from power deflation, repress moderates, appease moderates, or be intimidated. Now if the target, despite being powerful and self-righteous, has over-reacted, it has played into the hands of the terrorists. To avoid this, the target must not over-react. It is only through a knowledge of one's own perceptions and how they can be manipulated that one learns to avoid the propensity to make particular mistakes.

The terrorist's purpose is more than served the moment the media uses the phrase 'so-and-so city rocked by explosions', *'bomb visphoton se desh dahala'* or 'explosions rattle India', etc. **The terrorist aims for undue publicity and we unknowingly give it to him by overplaying his acts**. There is no way a modern large nation can prevent a terrorist from striking, whatever we may try; we can, however, learn to react in a more mature way.

8

70 Years of Indian Independence: Tapping the Untapped Potential

Sunil K Gulati*

Based on my 32 years experience in IAS as a sincere seeker here are the areas I feel we have huge untapped potential which we can and must release fast because undoubtedly the patience of people is running down and that is why they try to change government every five years. What are the untapped areas and could be the ways to tap that potential therein?

Firstiy amidst all the talk of e-commerce we forget that the rural houses almost all over India which host almost 70% population have still not been numbered and given a title document to show the ownership. Britishers during cadastral

* Proposed, in individual capacity, based on one's 32 years of service in IAS, by: Sunil K Gulati IAS, Vice-President AAPSI and Additional Chief Secretary, Haryana (mob: 09650334888, Email sunilaol@gmail.com, website: www.aapsiindia.org). Opinions given are purely personal and not official and aim is reforms and reducing corruption opportunities. Please feel free to call.

survey left the village homestead properties untouched marking them in a Lal Dora or red mark whereas rest of the land they made land records and title documents. For Boosting rural e-Commerce: **Permanent and Unique Property Numbers should be given for all village homestead properties** enabling computerized legal documentation of homestead land/rural house property. This will untap huge potential of rural homestead land and people will be able to easily mortgage the same (as they do for urban HUDA/DDA plots) and take loan for the education/business needs etc in a big way.

Secondly in rural areas, the perimeter defining the **Lal Dora or village homestead land** should be **revised suo motu every 20 years** by the Panchayat elected bodies themselves. Presently a structure outside the Lal Dora can be technically razed to the ground for non-complying with Town Planning laws regarding scheduled use of land. This leads to perpetual corruption and threat for such houses. The situation is worse for areas in the so-called 'Controlled Area' which is denied the autonomy of a village as well as the benefits of a town and ultimately breeds corruption due to lack of clear status. Census shows maximum urbanization of these Census towns. So special clear cut plans should be made for the Controlled Areas and Census Towns too to remove scope of ambiguity.

Third is the acute **need for rental housing** for **migrant workers who actually need accommodation** in the city/town where they work **and not a house as such**. So subsidized housing is misused/cornered by those with money power to invest in housing sector while the genuine needy remain unattended. Therefore, rental housing should be built for workforce and they should be allowed this facility at least in the first 10 years of their job. Later on the person can afford renting using HRA facility or build own house if necessary. The facility should be means tested. The rental can be charged to the escrow account of the company or the contractor with whom the worker is employed. A new Rental Housing Control Act should be made for ensuring success of Rental Housing Projects. This will check the rampant perpetual growth of slums as well. Similarly Start-up Housing/Rental Housing should be built for young/fresh skilled workforce using Labour Welfare Board funds etc and they should be allowed this facility at least in the first 10 years after passing out from first graduation/Vocational degree/diploma. The instalments can be collected through escrow account from employers.

Fourthly there is a **major need to boost EWS/LIG Housing** because research shows that the ratio of Service Providers to Service Consumers who reside in urban areas is almost 4:1. Accordingly we should fix a percentage of land (not plots) for the EWS/BPL/LIG houses. Present National Housing Policy indicates **20-25% of FAR be reserved for EWS/ LIG housing** but actually what is being given usually is 20-25% of plots **which actually comes to only 3-4% of the land** as usually EWS houses are just up to 300 sqft cnly (and not multistorey due to lack of Lifts) so the net impact is grossly inadequate and hence 99% of the shortage of housing is for this EWS/LIG category. Furthermore, to counter the problem, the FAR or FSI allowed should be double the normal rate for these categories. Subsidy for Lifts should be given or proceeds from the Labour Welfare Board should be used to give subsidized lift/stand-by power so critical for the survival of such a project. For EWS houses a major concern should be the travel cost, risk and time spent to reach workplace which denies the already weak person an opportunity to enhance the quality of her/his life. Therefore commercial non-polluting industrial or Service sector activity should be allowed at EWS/ LIG houses so that their travel woes can be reduced. So **mix use** (Residential + Commercial) should be allowed for these houses. Stress be laid on giving Semi-finished housing to the EWS/LIG so that they can contribute their own labour and build the insides of the house as per their need rather than 'one shoe fits all' approach currently in vogue. Aadhaar card should be made obligatory for identifying applicants to subsidized housing and also transfer of the same so that the misuse of facilities/Benami transactions and corruption can be checked and Housing reaches the poor needy. Actually most EWS housing is often cornered by fictitious persons. Housing within Industrial premises/complexes should be encouraged so as to ease mobility issues.

Fifthly our country needs desperately a **Technology Mission for New and Appropriate Technology for Housing** so as to changeover from earthen bricks which use up the precious topsoil of the earth to something that can build houses faster and cheaper using lesser of scarce land. The new technology should be demonstrated to win over the minds and hearts of EWS/LIG people who feel that they are being dished out 'inferior' houses in the garb of appropriate technology. The technology should be used to build all government buildings so as to instill consumer confidence. The skill sets for housing (plumbing, electrician, masonry etc) should be improved so that quality of housing improves and the House becomes a source of peace rather than a headache demanding maintenance all the time. In India building a house is normally a 2-3 years project while in most developed countries it takes just 3-6 months to get settled in own house.

Sixthly **Skilling up the Youth** so as to generate employment has to be the top priority of all States. In this regard the **Care Sector** offers immense scope of generating employment for at last 20 lakh people in the jobs of Caregiving for the Frail Elderly, for the Divyang persons needing care, Palliative Caregivers, Caregivers for the Drug addicts under rehabilitation and for the children. The very old (80+) is the fastest growing group in India at 3.6% PA as the life expectancy is going up, especially amongst the middle classes and upper class elderly and the non-communicable diseases (lifestyle diseases) are emerging as the leading cause of disability and death. These conditions of morbidity are prone to needing assisted living, especially at the later stages. Moreover with the Joint Family system is breaking down fast, especially in the middle class, which can afford separate housing and mobility, while the scope for intra-family support is rapidly declining, the need for **'assisted living for the elderly'** is picking up fast. Like Softwares, India is good at Soft skills and a Care Sector Skill development council needs to be set up which will promote certified care skill courses and get Aadhaar based background verification of caregivers done and promote jobs for Caregivers all over the world to make Indians the **'Caregivers of the World'**.

Seventh is the need of **Developing Human Values** in our citizens from the very beginning. It is a well known fact that 80-90% of the gross mental intelligence is formed within the initial 8-9 years and that is the most critical time for the parents to sow the right values in the child. Share of Children 0-14 years is almost 39% in total population and while the children are merely being clothed at home and fed (daily at Anganwadis) the window of opportunity that Anganwadis and early schools provide for Values development needs to be utilized urgently and sincerely. This is one of the major cause of ignorance and lack of attention towards Environment, Hygiene, Health, and Human Values resulting in poorer quality of life in the Rural domain/Slums. Training a child not to throw litter on the road can save 10,000 kg of litter from coming on the road in her/his lifetime. Same applies to being polite, respectful and non-abusive, especially towards women, which will prevent crime, road rage and crime against women later in life. Again simple things like washing hands and mouth at meals or bathing every day which can save huge burden on the health costs of the Nation. The need therefore is to invest in Software for Education i e better trained and locally resident Teachers as well Anganwadi Level Trainers who can entice children to schools and Anganwadis and keep them there and sow the Right seeds (SANSKARS) for a strong India, where every child will feel proud to be an Indian and also understand what being an Indian means. For this the Village Youth will be provided the know-how and do-how of such efforts and Trained to take charge of the children in their village and cultivate the VALUES in them early through 'HAMARE SANSKAR' Manual and audio-visual kits. The Rural/Slum/Suburban/Urban Youth Volunteers will become partners in Anganwadis and train the children in their/neighbouring areas on Human Values when they come for their daily feed at the Anganwadis. This programme can also be taken up in Primary Schools as daily special sessions. Such Youth will need about one month training course and can be paid an honorarium of about ₹4,000 PM (if part time and ₹8,000 PM if full time) which can be given from ICDS/Labour Welfare Cess or NREGA. The Project can use latest IEC (Information, Education and Communication) Tools and Costs involved in the Project will only be VCDs, pamphlets, and the Cost of Trainer's Honorarium etc. Motorcycles can be refitted so that Motorcycle Engine dynamo be used as Generator to power Overhead Projectors which can be used to beat the power problem nationwide.

In USA we find the following 12 values being taught in a Special, Systematic way to be instilled in the children of Primary/Middle School with one value being the topic of each month and all students contributing to imbibing the same. The values as they are defined show how the foundations of a strong nation can be made:

1. **Respect:** Courteous Consideration and High Regard for Others
2. **Honesty:** A sense of Honour, truthfulness, integrity, and sincerity
3. **Courage:** The power to face difficulties, obstacles, and challenges
4. **Gratitude:** Thankfulness expressed by acknowledged appreciation
5. **Generosity:** Unselfishness demonstrated by caring, concern and sharing.
6. **Responsibility**: Cooperation, perseverance, self-discipline and good citizenship.
7. **Caring:** Attention and concern for the welfare and needs of others through both words and actions

8. **Knowledge:** Awareness of facts, truths and principles through critical and creative thinking processes.
9. **Fairness:** Equity, equality and consistency applied in ALL Situations.
10. **Patriotism:** good citizenship displaying high regard for laws, government and the heritage of one's country.
11. **Service:** Helpfulness exhibited by useful productivity.
12. **Courtesy:** Polite behaviour and excellence in manners in social conduct.

Accordingly a Trainer's Manual 'The HAMARE SANSKAR MANUAL' which is basically designed to train a trainer on how to sow basic human values in children up to mental age of 8 years (physical age could be up to 14 years) has been prepared. This is intended to be a 15 days programme for pre-school (Anganwadis) and Junior classes of the village/Slum school on a 90 minutes daily basis. Or it can be taken up for 60 minutes daily for 30 days. Group size should be 30-35 preferably. At the same time the Volunteers (young or old) available on part time basis can be given a copy of the Manual to work with the children.

Eighth would be furthering 'Beti Bachao Beti Padhao' through **Raising Status of Women.** This project will work on Raising Status of Women by making the presence of Women visible by making Girls Hostel for students in each district town/near major colleges and removing drudgery from the so called women oriented roles such as cooking by providing LPG in every house, fetching water by providing clean water at each doorstep, toilet and bathroom in every house besides an electricity point and opening bank accounts of all women.

Ninth would be **Recognizing National Service done by Youth** with Credits and Gap year because there is so much to do for the country for which we can constructively engage Youth, such as caring for elderly, hygiene campaigns, Human Values campaign or Social Service works. But the youth must get recognition in return. This can be done by giving credits in the academic record for genuine social work done by youth and recognizing GAP YEAR as a legitimate and respected activity in the Academic Record all over India.

Tenth Project would be the **National Oral Hygiene Campaign** which can easily piggy back on the Human Values Project team except that this will go on during the day by Targeting all schools. Oral hygiene is the starting point of all hygiene, and thus healthy way of life. This project will also motivate each non-smoker to motivate at least one smoker to give up smoking. Similarly a strong campaign to highlight harmful effects of tobacco chewing, alcohol and drugs will be taken up.

Eleventh project is **Tapping Sports Power of India**. The idea is to have trained and accomplished sportspersons take charge of boys and girls in each village and *kasba* of India and train them (1M+1F trainer per 1,000 population) in all kinds of Sports daily round the year. Ultimate aim is to make India Indian youth healthy and work as a team and finally make India into a sports superpower. Funding could be from NAREGA/Labour welfare fund/CSR fund of corporates etc

Twelfth project is **Tapping the World Art Market** because India has so much cultural diversity and millions of Artists (Painters and Sculptors) but they are not getting enough market to practice Art as a respectable profession. Various Zonal Cultural Centres and Kala Akademies must open Kala Haats in each nook and corner of the country in large towns and cities and the Haats (Markets) must locate, document and book or buy and keep art and put it up for ONLINE sale so that buyers and government departments can see online and buy the Art directly eliminating the middlemen and the need for three quotations to buy Art. We can make promotion of Art a part of Corporate Social Responsibility Activity which can be promoted through corporates the world over so that India can capture the world market which has got dominated by China which has over 90% just one tribe (Han) as against so much cultural diversity in India.

Finally we must launch a **Nationwide Endeavour for Tackling High Fertility** because once we exceed our Carrying capacity, the socio-economic burden of population itself can become a serious issue. For this, especially in the high fertility States, we must work seriously on making youth aware of family size and fertility issues by discussions on "Carrying Capacity" of each village, town, slum and inhabitation. Efforts should be to promote the idea among Youth of achieving **'Self-Sufficiency before Marriage'** by acquiring necessary skills and space to earn and run a household first. All parents can be motivated to enjoy life through Birth Spacing, use of Contraceptives etc.

Biggest crisis that Governance in India faces today is – Governance of Human Resources. We must start involving the officers by asking them which area they would like to contribute the best, and give them the responsibility accordingly. Once the inner (personal) goals and the organizational goals are oriented in the same direction, progress is bound to grow exponentially. A strong Feedback loop is required in the government so as to be able to identify and reward the performers punish the non-performers so that people do not continue to suffer....

9

India Marches Ahead

Vivek Garg

DEMOCRACY

Strong democratic institutions have been another achievement of India. Inspite of various pulls and pressures of a new and poor nation at its independence, India has been able to develop its democracy beautifully by giving universal franchise to its citizens irrespective of their economic and social status. India has remained an island of democracy amid a vast ocean of autocratic rules in the neighbourhood. India has been a pulsating, throbbing democracy and has emerged as the largest democracy in the world. Right from the days of Pandit Jawaharlal Nehru and Sardar Vallabhbhai Patel, when the two topmost Indian leaders often differed drastically from each other on core issues, to the contemporary times of Anna Hazare, India has continued on the democratic path. Whenever a general election has thrown out a government, the new dispensation has taken over peacefully, many a times.

EDUCATION

Education in India is provided by the public sector as well as the private sector, with control and funding coming from three levels: Central, State and local. Under various articles of the Indian Constitution, free and compulsory education is provided as a fundamental right to children between the ages of 6 and 14. The ratio of public schools to private schools in India is 7:5. As per the Annual Status of Education Report (ASER) 2012, 96.5% of all rural children between the ages of 6-14 were enrolled in school. This is the fourth annual survey to report enrolment above 96%. Another report from 2013 stated that there were 22.9 crore students enrolled in different accredited urban and rural schools of India, from Class I to XII, representing an increase of 23 lakh students over 2002 total enrolment, and a 19% increase in girl's enrolment. The number of literate women among the female population of India was between 2-6% from the British Raj onwards to the formation of an independent India. Concerted efforts led to improvement from 15.3% in 1961 to 28.5% in 1981. By 2001 literacy for women had exceeded 50% of the overall female population, though these statistics were still very low compared to world standards and even male literacy within India.

Pulling itself out from widespread illiteracy, India has managed to bring its education system at par with the global standard. The number of schools witnessed a dramatic increase during the post-independence era. The Parliament made elementary education a fundamental right for children in the age group of 6-14 years by passing the 86th amendment to the Constitution in 2002. At independence, India's literacy rate was a paltry 12.2% which increased to 74.04% in 2011.

The Government launched the Sarva Siksha Abhiyan in 2001 to ensure education for the children from 6 to 14 years. Prior to that, it had launched an effective initiative – Sponsored District Education Programme, which increased the number of schools across the country. In a bid to attract children to schools, especially in the rural areas, the government also started implementing the mid-day meals programme in 1995.

Indian Institute of Technology (IITs) play a vital role in India's social and economic development. IITs are among India's most elite engineering institutions. Indian Institutes of Technology (IITs) are autonomous public institutes of higher education. The Institutes of Technology Act, 1961 lists twenty-three institutes located at Bhilai, Madras, Delhi, Dhanbad, Dharwad, Goa, Guwahati, Jammu, Kanpur, Kharagpur, Bombay, Roorkee, Bhubaneswar, Gandhinagar, Hyderabad, Indore, Jodhpur, Mandi, Palghat, Patna, Ropar, Tirupati and Varanasi. Some of the following IITians have taken India by a storm in the past few years and managed to make a mark in almost every profession we can think of under the sun:

1. Sundar Pichai – Bachelor of Metallurgical Engineering, IIT Kharagpur (Chief Executive Officer of Google).
2. NR Narayana Murthy – MTech, IIT Kanpur (Co-founder and ex-Chairman of Infosys).
3. Sachin Bansal – Bachelor of Computer Science, IIT Delhi (Co-founder of Flipkart).
4. Vinod Khosla – Bachelor of Electrical Engineering, IIT Delhi (Co-founder of Sun Microsystems).
5. Nikesh Arora – Bachelor of Electrical Engineering, IIT (BHU) Varanasi (Ex-President and COO of SoftBank Corp).

6. Amit Singhal – Bachelor of Computer Science, IIT Roorkee (Senior Vice-President of Engineering at Uber).
7. Chetan Bhagat – Bachelor of Mechanical Engineering, IIT Delhi (Author, Columnist, Screenwriter, Television Personality and Motivational Speaker).
8. Manohar Parrikar – Bachelor of Metallurgical Engineering, IIT Bombay (former Defence Minister of India, Chief Minister of Goa).
9. Rajat Gupta – Bachelor of Mechanical Engineering, IIT Delhi (Managing Director (former chief executive McKinsey & Company, former board member of corporations including Goldman Sachs, Procter & Gamble, American Airlines, former advisor to non-profits such as the Bill & Melinda Gates Foundation and The Global Fund to Fight AIDS, Tuberculosis and Malaria).
10. Jayant Sinha – Bachelor of Technology, IIT Delhi (Minister of State for Civil Aviation).
11. Raghuram Rajan – Bachelor of Electrical Engineering, IIT Delhi (former Governor of the Reserve Bank of India).

National Institute of Technology (NITs) are a group of premier federally-funded public engineering institutes in India. These institutions have been declared as Institutes of National Importance alongside the Indian Institutes of Technology (IITs) by an Act of Parliament of India. These institutes of national importance receive special recognition and funding from the Government of India. The NIT Council is the supreme governing body of India's National Institutes of

Technology (NIT) system. All 31 NITs are funded by the Government of India. These institutes are among the top ranked engineering colleges in India.

Indian Institute of Information Technology (IIITs), set up, funded and managed by Ministry of Human Resource Development. The centrally funded institution of technical and science education has five IIITs at Allahabad, Gwalior, Jabalpur, Kancheepuram and Kurnool. The addition of new IIITs as Institutes of National Importance was proposed under the Indian Institutes of Information Technology Bill 2010. This bill, renamed as IIIT Bill 2014, was passed by the Parliament on December 1, 2014, thus granting the status of Institutes of National Importance upon the four IIITs in Allahabad, Gwalior, Jabalpur and Kancheepuram. The other IIITs are set up on the public-private partnership (PPP) model, funded by the central government, state governments and industry partners in the ratio 50:35:15. Indian Institutes of Information Technology (IIITs) are a group of institutes of higher education in India, focused on information technology. They are established, funded and managed by the Ministry of Human Resource Development. Government is likely to approve the Indian Institute of Information Technology (IIIT) Bill that seeks to give IIITs administrative autonomy and uniformity and set up 20 more such schools on a public-private partnership (PPP) model. Admissions into undergraduate programmes in IIITs are through the Joint Entrance Examination JEE/GATE.

All India Institute of Medical Sciences (AIIMSs) are a group of autonomous public medical colleges of higher education. AIIMS New Delhi, the fore-runner parent excellence institution, was established in 1956. The second campus of AIIMS New Delhi (AIIMS-II), spread over 330 acres of land was visualized by Government of India in 2009 at Badhsa village in Haryana's Jhajjar district. AIIMS-II is to be developed as the largest Medical Education centre for super-specialities in the world. Its beginning was launched on 30th May 2012. IIT Delhi is also planning to set up an extension near the proposed AIIMS. The new campus will be collaborating with AIIMS in the fields of Biological Science, Pharmacology and Chemical Engineering. Government is also planning to open National Cancer Institute within the campus of AIIMS Jhajjar. Former President of India asked to develop AIIMS like Institutions in other parts of the country linked with AIIMS Delhi. President of AIIMS said that 6 AIIMS will be started shortly. Following are the upcoming and planned AIIMS: AIIMS Changsari, Assam; AIIMS Bihar, AIIMS Himachal Pradesh; AIIMS Bathinda, Punjab; AIIMS Jammu, Jammu and Kashmir; AIIMS Srinagar, Jammu and Kashmir; AIIMS Gorakhpur, Uttar Pradesh; AIIMS Rae Bareli, Uttar Pradesh; AIIMS Kalyani, West Bengal; AIIMS Mangalagiri, Andhra Pradesh; AIIMS Tamil Nadu; AIIMS Deoghar, Jharkhand; AIIMS Rajkot, Gujarat; AIIMS Nagpur, Maharashtra.

Development of Technical Education

Since independence, India has been developing its technical education sector steadfastly. This resulted into our green revolution which increased our foodgrain production more than four times, our independent space programmes, eradication of epidemics and our envious IT sector. We are virtually largest exporters of engineers today. Taking into account the mammoth size of India, its demography and poverty and plunder left behind by colonial powers at the time of independence, Indians have been achieving marvellously good results.

GROWTH OF AGRICULTURAL SECTOR

Since 1950s, the progress in agriculture has been somewhat steady. India was importer of foodgrains and depended upon international food aid up to mid-1960s. India faced severe drought in 1965 and 1966 and were recipient of food aid under PL-480 act of US government. The sector grew at about 1 per cent per annum in the first half of the 20th century. During the post-Independence era, the growth rate nudged about 2.6 per cent per annum. Expansion of farming area and introduction of high-yielding varieties of crops were the major factors of growth in agricultural production. The sector could manage to end dependency on imported foodgrains. It has progressed both in terms of yield and structural changes. Consistent investment in research, land reforms, expansion of scope for credit facilities, and improvement in rural infrastructure were some other determining factors that brought about an agricultural revolution in the country. However since then lot of scenario changed due to significant policy reforms and green revolution in India. Today, India has self-sufficiency in food production and exports various foodgrains. We are the largest producers of fruits, milk, oilseeds, sunflower seeds and second largest producers of wheat, rice, sugarcane, potato, tea, cotton etc in the world. In addition to growth in total output, agriculture in India has shown an increase in average output per acre since independence. While our total population tripled since independence, our foodgrain production more than quadrupled and there has been substantial increase in available foodgrain per capita. The country has also grown strong in the agri-biotech sector. The Rabobank report reveals that the agri-biotech sector has been growing at 30 per cent since the last few years. The country is also likely to become a major producer of genetically modified/engineered crops.

RIGHT TO FOOD

The right to food is enshrined in the Indian Constitution, Article 47 (Duty of the State to raise the level of nutrition and the standard of living and to improve public health):

"The State shall regard the raising of the level of nutrition and the standard of living of its people and the improvement of public health as among its primary duties and, in particular, the State shall endeavour to bring about prohibition of the consumption except for medicinal purpose of intoxicating drinks and of drugs which are injurious to health."

Fifty per cent of the world's hungry live in India, with 200 million food-insecure people in 2008 according to the FAO. India ranks 66th out of 88 nations on the Global Hunger Index.

In 2001, India's Supreme Court recognized the right to food, transforming policy choices into enforceable rights. The case started with a written petition submitted to the Supreme Court in April 2001 by the People's Union for Civil Liberties, Rajasthan, leading to prolonged public interest litigation. Moreover, a larger public Right to Food Campaign is founded.

In 2011, the National Food Security Bill, 2011, popularly known as Right to Food Bill was proposed. In 2013, National Food Security Act, 2013 was passed by the Indian Parliament.

The Act guarantees subsidised food to 50% of the urban population and 75% of the rural population. The proposed legislation would provide rice, wheat and coarse grain at very low prices to 'priority households' similar to Below Poverty Line families. Distribution will be through the current Public Distribution System, a government-run ration and fair price shops.

"India provides one of the best examples in the world in terms of the justiciability of the right to food. The Constitution of India prohibits discrimination and recognizes all human rights. The right to life is recognized as a directly justiciable fundamental right (Article 21), while the right to food is defined as a directive principle of State policy (Article 47). As it has interpreted these provisions, the Supreme Court of India has found that the Government has a constitutional obligation to take steps to fight hunger and extreme poverty and to ensure a life with dignity for all individuals."

SPACE PROGRAMMES

Indians have been able to develop one of the most envious space programmes in the world started in the year 1969 after independence. India's modest efforts to conquer the space that began with the successful launch of its first satellite Aryabhatta in 1975 have now come of age.

Aryabhatta was launched by India on 19 April 1975 from Kapustin Yar, a Russian rocket. It was built to gain experience in building and operating a satellite in space. The launch came from an agreement signed in 1972 between India and the Soviet Union.

Chandrayan was India's first lunar probe. It was launched in October 2008, and operated until August 2009. India launched the spacecraft using a PSLV-XL rocket on 22 October 2008 from Satish Dhawan Space Centre, Sriharikota, Andhra Pradesh. Prime Minister Atal Bihari Vajpayee announced the project on course in his Independence Day speech on 15 August 2003. India researched and developed its own technology in order to explore the Moon.

Today we are launching various space programmes including Lunar and Mars mission, and commercial launching of satellites of developed nations at very low cost. We have benefited humanity by way of forecasting of cyclones in Indian peninsula thereby substantially reducing loss of life due to our space programmes.

November 5, 2013 was marked as one of the most significant days in Indian history. With the lift-off of **Mars Orbiter Mission** spacecraft, India's first interplanetary mission was executed. The spacecraft lifted off from Satish Dhawan Space Centre, Sriharikota, Andhra Pradesh. Mangalyan entered Mars orbit on September 24, 2014, making India the first Asian country and only the fourth country in the world to enter the Mars orbit in its first attempt. Mars Orbiter Mission's objective is to collect data from the red planet and also showcase India's rocket launch systems, spacecraft-building and operations capabilities. The total cost of the mission was approximately US $73 million, making it the least-expensive Mars mission to date.

India is among the select few space powers in the world to launch foreign satellites and eye a big chunk of the $200 billion commercial rocket launch industry. India has sewn up space agreements with over 20 countries. It is no mean achievement for a country that was finding it difficult to feed its own people till it successfully embarked on a Green Revolution nearly half a century ago, is now aiming literally for the stars! In May 2016, the ISRO achieved another milestone with the successful launch of the Reusable Launch Vehicle – Technology Demonstrator. The reusable vehicle will enable the ISRO to save nearly 80 per cent of mission costs in future. But the RLVs will be operationalised only by 2030.

On 15th February 2017, ISRO successfully launched the **Polar Satellite Launch Vehicle** C37 into orbit. The rocket launched 104 satellites of which three are Indian, 88 are from the USA and the rest from Germany, Israel, Kazakhstan, the Netherlands, Switzerland, and the United Arab Emirates. The PSLV-C37 cost around $15 million to launch. In comparison, it costs SpaceX roughly $60 million to do the same. NASA used to spend $100 million to send satellites into space, a cost so high that they found SpaceX to be a far lucrative offer. India, of all the space-capable nations, has the lowest cost for sending satellites into space. Former ISRO Chairman G Madhavan Nair said, "This is no new technology. We (Indian Space Research Organisation) started with ten satellites (on board a single rocket), then went to 18 or something; then it's 35. Now it's 104. If you make 3 or 4 kg satellite, it (PSLV) can take 300 to 400 satellites at a time."

At the foundation day ceremony of the Raja Ramanna Centre for Advanced Technology, AS Kiran Kumar, Chairman of Indian Space Research Organisation (ISRO) said that India has the capability to develop a space station. "We still talk about what would be the immediate benefits of a manned space mission," Kumar said. "That is why the country has not made up its mind about when to invest in a space station," he said.

Prime Minister Narendra Modi's pet **South Asian satellite project** will be launched in March 2017. The South Asian satellite will be a part of GSAT-9, which will be launched in March this year. The communication satellite was scheduled to be launched in December 2016, but was slightly delayed as some other satellites were to be launched before that. Talks with Afghanistan to have the country on-board for the project is in its final stages. Apart from India, the satellite will benefit Sri Lanka, Maldives, Bangladesh, Nepal and Bhutan.

INDEPENDENT FOREIGN POLICY

After India gained independence from the United Kingdom in 1947, it soon joined the Commonwealth of Nations and strongly supported independence movements in other colonies, like the Indonesian National Revolution. During the Cold War, India adopted a foreign policy of not aligning itself with any major power bloc. However, India developed close ties with the Soviet Union and received extensive military support from it. India's foreign policy has always regarded the concept of neighbourhood as one of widening concentric circles, around a central axis of historical and cultural commonalities. India has been able to pursue an independent foreign policy after independence and interference by outside powers have been zero, due to strides made by India in various fields like agriculture production, economic progress, space programmes, nuclear energy and defence. End of Cold War significantly affected India's foreign policy, as it did for much of the world. The country now seeks to strengthen its diplomatic and economic ties with the United States, the European Union, Japan, Israel, Mexico, and Brazil. India has also forged close ties with the member states of the Association of Southeast Asian Nations, African Union, Arab League and Iran. Though India continues to have a military relationship with Russia, Israel has emerged as India's second largest military partner while India has built a strong strategic partnership with the United States. The foreign policy of Narendra Modi indicated a shift towards focusing on the Asian region and, more broadly, trade deals.

INDIAN ARMED FORCES

Indians have learnt lessons from history very well and focused their energy in developing strong deterrent in the form of their armed forces. India is one of four largest military powers in the world today and has got one of the most sophisticated missile programmes in the world. Indian armed forces consists of three professional uniformed services: Indian Army, Indian Navy, and Indian Air Force. Additionally, the Indian Armed Forces are supported by Indian Coast Guard and paramilitary organisations (Assam Rifles and Special Frontier Force) and various inter-service commands and institutions such as the Strategic Forces Command, the Andaman and Nicobar Command and the Integrated Defence Staff. The President of India is the Supreme Commander of the Indian armed forces. The Indian Armed Forces are under the management of the Ministry of Defence (MoD). It is world's 3rd largest military force and has the world's largest volunteer army. Indian armed forces have been engaged in a number of major military operations, including the Indo-Pakistani wars of 1947, 1965 and 1971, the Kargil War, and the Siachen conflict among others. India honours its armed forces and military personnel annually on Armed Forces Flag Day, 7 December. Since 1962, the IAF has maintained close military relations with Russia, including cooperative development on programmes such as the Fifth Generation Fighter Aircraft (FGFA) and the Multirole Transport Aircraft (MTA). Armed with nuclear triad, Indian armed forces are steadily undergoing modernisation, with investments in areas such as futuristic soldier systems and missile defence system. Department of Defence Production of the Ministry of Defence is responsible for the indigenous production of equipment used by the Indian armed forces. It comprises 41 Ordnance Factories under control of the Ordnance Factories Board and 8 Defence PSUs namely, HAL, BEL, BEML, BDL, MDL, GSL, GRSE and Midhani. India was the largest importer of defence equipment in 2014 with Russia, Israel, France and the United States being the top foreign suppliers of military equipment. Government of India has launched Make in India initiative to indigenise manufacturing and reduce dependence on imports, including defence imports and procurement.

GROWING ECONOMY

India is the leading economy of the decade and the role is quite mesmerizing and demanding. With a historical trend of increasing growth rate Indian market has always been a potential area for creation of new jobs. There a number of reasons which have led India to this very stage involving decisions of precise and decisive nature. The Economist Intelligence Unit (EIU), the research and analysis division of The Economist Group in its global economic outlook said that India continues to be the fastest-growing large economy beating China.

"We expect GDP to grow at 7.1 per cent year-on-year in 2017-18, up from 6.3 per cent in 2016-17, as the country gets sufficiently remonetised, and consumption moves back to pre-demonetisation levels," HSBC India Chief Economist Pranjul Bhandari said.

The Gross Domestic Product (GDP) in India expanded 1.80 per cent in the third quarter of 2016 over the previous quarter. GDP Growth Rate in India averaged 1.67 per cent from 1996 until 2016, reaching an all time high of 5.80 per cent in the second quarter of 2009 and a record low of –1.80 per cent in the first quarter of 2009.

FASTEST GROWING SERVICES SECTOR

A major development in the nation's services sector has been the tele services and information technology. A trend that started some two decades back is now well in its prime. Several multinational firms continue to outsource their tele services and IT services to India. The acquisition of expertise in information technology has led to the generation of thousands of new jobs, which in turn increased domestic consumption and naturally, more foreign direct investments happened to meet the demands. Presently, the services sector employs 23 per cent of the Indian workforce and this process of development started back in the 1980s. In the 60s, the sector employed only 4.5 per cent of the working population. According to the Central Statistical Organization, the services sector accounted for 63 per cent of Indian GDP in 2008 and the figure continues to grow.

India has the second fastest growing services sector with its compound annual growth rate at 9 per cent, just below China's 10.9 per cent, during the last 11-year period from 2001 to 2012, the Economic Survey for 2013-14 said. Russia at 5.4 per cent is a distant third. Among the world's top 15 countries in terms of GDP, India ranked 10th in terms of overall GDP and 12th in terms of services GDP in 2012. As per the survey, in India, the growth of services-sector GDP has been higher than that of overall GDP between the period 2001-2014. Services constitute a major portion of India's GDP with a 57 per cent share in GDP at factor cost (at current prices) in 2013-14, an increase of 6 percentage points over 2000-01. Despite deceleration, services GDP growth at 6.8 per cent was above the 4.7 per cent overall GDP growth in 2013-14. India's share in world services exports, which increased from 0.6 per cent in 1990 to 1.1 per cent in 2000 and further to 3.3 per cent in 2013, has been increasing faster than its share in world merchandise exports, according to the survey. However, moving in tandem with global exports of financial services, India's exports of financial services registered a high growth of 34.4 per cent in 2013-14.

INFRASTRUCTURE DEVELOPMENT

As India needs power to drive its growth engine, it has triggered a noteworthy improvement in the availability of energy by adopting a multi-pronged approach. After almost seven decades of Independence, India has emerged as the third largest producer of electricity in Asia. It has increased its electricity generation capacity from 1,362 MW in 1947 to 1,13,506 MW as of 2004. Overall, power generation in India has increased from 301 billion units (BUs) during 1992-93 to 558.1 BUs in 2003-04. When it comes to rural electrification, the Indian government has managed to bring lights to 5,93,732 (2013 figures) villages as compared to 3,061 in 1950. The Indian road network has become one of the largest in the world with the total road length increasing from 0.399 million km in 1951 to 4.24 million km as of July 2014. Moreover, the total length of the country's national highways has increased from 24,000 km (1947-69) to 92,851 km (2014). Governmental efforts have led to the expansion of the network of State highways and major district roads, which in turn has directly contributed to industrial growth.

WOMEN EMPOWERMENT

India grew up to be a nation, who elected woman as Speaker, Prime Minister and President, unlike the greatest power in the world, the United States of America. We even had four major States to appoint women CM, so also Leader of Opposition. Based on the ideas championed by our founding fathers for women empowerment, many social, economic and political provisions were incorporated in the Indian Constitution. Women in India now participate in areas such as education, sports, politics, media, art and culture, service sector and science and technology.

Politicians

Indira Gandhi: Former Prime Minister of India for 11 years.

Pratibha Patil: President of India (12th) from 2007 to 2012.

Sumitra Mahajan: Speaker of the 16th Lok Sabha. She belongs to Bharatiya Janata Party.

Sushma Swaraj: Minister of External Affairs, Leader of Opposition in Lok Sabha (2009-2014).

Nirmala Sitharaman: Minister of State (Independent Charge) for Commerce and Industry.

Vasundhara Raje: Chief Minister of Rajasthan.

Mamata Banerjee: Chief Minister of West Bengal.

Mehbooba Mufti: Chief Minister of Jammu and Kashmir

Jurists

M Fathima Beevi: Judge (1989-1992) of the Supreme Court of India.

Leila Seth: Chief Justice (1991-1996) of Himachal Pradesh High Court.

Sujata Vasant Manohar: Judge (1994-1999) of the Supreme Court of India.

Rekha Manharlal Doshit: Chief Justice (2010-2014) of Patna High Court, Bihar.

Administrators

Arundhati Bhattacharya: Chairperson, State Bank of India.

Chanda Kochhar: MD, CEO, ICICI Bank.

Indra K Nooyi: Chairperson and CEO of PepsiCo.

Astronauts

Kalpana Chawla: First Indian woman to go to space. Kalpana Chawla was one of the seven crew members that died in the Space Shuttle Columbia disaster.

Sunita Williams: American astronaut and United States Navy officer of Indian-Slovenian descent. Time spent in space: 321 days 17 hours 15 minutes.

Entrepreneur

Nita Ambani: Chairperson, Reliance Foundation and Director, Reliance Industries.

Sports

Sania Mirza is an international tennis player.

Saina Nehwal is an international badminton singles player.

PV Sindhu is a professional badminton player. At the 2016 Summer Olympics, she became the first Indian woman to win an Olympic silver medal.

Persons of Indian Origin

Nimrata 'Nikki' Haley Randhawa: She easily won confirmation to be President Donald Trump's ambassador to the United Nations.

Seema Verma (Dr): US President-elect Donald Trump nominated (Dr) Seema Verma to a top administration position, putting her in charge of a federal agency within the health department as part of a 'dream team' which he said would transform America's healthcare system.

RELIGIOUS TOLERANCE

India is one of the most diverse nations in terms of religion, it being the birthplace of four major world religions: Hinduism, Jainism, Buddhism and Sikhism. Even though Hindus form close to 80 percent of the population, India also has region-specific religious practices: for instance, Jammu and Kashmir has a Muslim majority, Punjab has a Sikh majority, Nagaland, Meghalaya and Mizoram have Christian majorities and the

Indian Himalayas such as Sikkim and Darjeeling, Ladakh, Arunachal Pradesh and the State of Maharashtra have large concentrations of Buddhist population. The country has significant Muslim, Sikh, Christian, Buddhist, Jain and Zoroastrian populations. Islam is the largest minority religion in India, and the Indian Muslims form the third largest Muslim population in the world, accounting for over 14 per cent of the nation's population. Despite having such diversity in terms of religions and cultures, and many elements working round the clock to create disturbance among them, our nation remains by far the largest one to have people living peacefully with each other. The Preamble of the Indian Constitution has the word 'secular', thereby implying that the State will not discriminate, patronise or meddle in the profession of any religion. However, it shields individual religions or groups by adding religious rights as fundamental rights. Article 25 says "all persons are equally entitled to freedom of conscience and the right to freely profess, practice, and propagate religion subject to public order, morality and health." Further, Article 26 says that all denominations can manage their own affairs in matters of religion. All these rights are subject to be regulated by the State. Some major religious holidays like Christmas (Christian), Eid (Muslim), Guru Nanak's birth anniversary (Sikh) and Holi (Hindu) are considered national holidays. Private schools offering religious instruction are permitted while government schools are non-religious. Article 25 of the Indian Constitution is a basic human right guarantee that cannot be subverted or misinterpreted in any manner. It is in this context that the anti-conversion laws in India must be viewed. Anti-conversion laws are promulgated on the premise that forced or induced conversions happen and need to be prevented. Supreme Court supported the laws saying, "What is freedom for one is freedom for the other in equal measure and there can, therefore, be no such thing as a fundamental right to convert any person to one's own religion."

HEALTHCARE

A decrease in death rates is considered one of the major achievements that came India's way in this sector. While life expectancy was around 37 years in 1951, it almost doubled to 65 years by 2011. Infant mortality has also seen a marked decline with death rate coming down to half of what it was during the 50s. Similar improvement was noticed in maternal mortality rate also.

After a long-drawn struggle, India has finally been declared a polio-free country. Malnutrition in children under five years came down to 44% in 2006 from 67% in 1979. Government's efforts yielded result as the number of tuberculosis cases also got reduced to 185 per lakh people in 2009. The cases of HIV-infected people are also witnessing a declining trend. Besides increased public health spending (about 6% of the GDP), the government has launched a series of ambitious initiatives including 'Healthcare for all by 2020' and distribution of free medicines to the people falling under lowest-income group.

Eradication of Epidemics and Polio

We have successfully eradicated various epidemics and Polio from our nation. Life expectancy is 68.89 years which was only 32 years at the time of independence. In March 2014, the World Health Organisation certified the South-East Asian region – which includes India, a polio free region. WHO presented official certification to India for its 'Polio Free' status. This is one of the major achievement taking into account that we comprise 17% of world population.

SCIENTIFIC ACHIEVEMENTS

Independent India has taken confident strides in its road to scientific development. Its prowess is being manifested in a gradual scaling up of ambitious projects. India takes pride in its space programmes, which began with the launch of its first satellite Aryabhatta in 1975. Since then, India has emerged as a space power that has successfully launched foreign satellites. Its first mission to Mars was launched in November 2013 which successfully reached the planet's orbit on 24 September 2014.

India is also aggressively pursuing both nuclear and missile programmes. That has simultaneously augmented the country's defence strength as well. BrahMos inducted into the defence system is the world's fastest cruise missile that has been jointly developed by India and Russia. After more than six decades of independence, India has now come closer to being an independent force to reckon with in the field of nuclear and missile technology.

Nuclear and Missile Programmes

No other programmes have beefed up India's defence and forced the world to acknowledge India's strides in the field of defence and science and technology as these two. India's prowess in the field of missile technology is a strong deterrent for the enemies.

The nuclear programme and the missile programme form an integral part of this. India has been running the two programmes simultaneously and successfully. India's missile programme is spearheaded by such missile systems as the Agni, Prithvi, Akash and Nag. BrahMos, the world's fastest Cruise missile jointly developed by India and Russia, is the latest addition to the Indian missile programme. According Sputnik, a Russian news agency, as many as seven countries from the Asia and the Pacific, Latin America and the Middle East are keeping a close eye on the trials of BrahMos on the Su-30 MKI. BrahMos Aerospace spokesperson Praveen Pathak said, "We have requests from seven countries in Asia and the Pacific, Latin America and the Middle East, which already have Su-30s." Pathak further said that once the test-firing trials from Su-30 MKI were complete, many of these countries would line up to buy the missile.

SHIFT IN INDIAN POLITICS

Bharatiya Janata Party came to prominence in 1990s when it emerged as a ruling party at the national level. It was founded in 1980, however its legacy has been traced back to the Bharatiya Jan Sangh (1951) and Rashtriya Swayamsevek Sangh (RSS) (1925). After the 1998 general election, the BJP-led coalition known as the National Democratic Alliance (NDA) formed government under Prime Minister Atal Bihari Vajpayee for a year. Following fresh elections, the NDA government, again headed by Atal Bihari Vajpayee, lasted for a full term in office; this was the first non-Congress government to do so.

New India – 2014 General Election

In the 2014 Indian general election, the BJP won 282 seats, leading the NDA to a tally of 336 seats in the 543-seat Lok

Sabha. Narendra Modi was sworn in as the 15th Prime Minister of India on 26 May 2014. Since that election, Modi leads the NDA government as Prime Minister and as of March 2017, the alliance governs 17 States. Political analysts have suggested several reasons for this victory, including the popularity of Modi, and the loss of support for the Congress due to the corruption scandals. Most commentators seem to agree that May 2014 marks an historic moment. One reason is the scale of Modi's landslide victory, which scooped up 282 seats for the BJP and thus an absolute majority in parliament. That is first time since 1984 that any party has won a majority for itself. It is also the first time ever that a party other than Congress has done so. Conversely, the defeat for Congress is far worse than anything in its long history of dominating Indian politics: it won fewer than a sixth the seats of its rival, getting just 44. In much of north India, the political heartland, Congress was wiped out. The immense dissatisfaction with Congress was undeniable. Voters were unhappy with high inflation, slowing growth, weak leadership and corruption. This suggests an important shift in Indian politics. The BJP did extraordinarily well because it approached the election in a far more professional, strategic and efficient way than its rivals. More than 60 per cent of the country's population now lives in States either ruled by the BJP alone or in partnership. The stunning Uttar Pradesh victory also means the BJP controls three of the four original BIMARU States, which are now the country's fastest-growing, as well as States that are hubs of industrial activity (including Gujarat, Maharashtra, Uttarakhand and Andhra Pradesh). Latest statistics released by McKinsey & Co project India's growth over the next decade to be led primarily by eight high-performing States – Gujarat,

Haryana, Maharashtra, Andhra Pradesh, Telangana, Tamil Nadu, Himachal Pradesh and Uttarakhand. Five of these are in the NDA fold, while only one is under Congress rule now.

In the end the 2014 election was about 'chappan inch ki chaati', a politician having a massive 56 inch chest hailing from Vadnagar in Gujarat. Narendra Modi re-invented the BJP. This was almost a new freshly minted BJP, market friendly, not pushing swadeshi economics. As the Lotus party's Prime Ministerial nominee Modi had chosen Varanasi, one of the holiest pilgrim centres for the Hindus. It is generally believed that all roads from UP lead to the seat of power on the Raisina Hill in the imposing South Block in New Delhi. Verdict 2014 has placed India at the cusp of change. Narendra Modi has redefined the idea of New India and the way it is to be governed.

Major Twist – 2017 Uttar Pradesh and Uttarakhand Assembly Elections

The assembly polls are being seen as a referendum on Prime Minister Narendra Modi's popularity and his reforms agenda, particularly demonetisation. Bharatiya Janata Party has won stunning election victories in Uttar Pradesh and Uttarakhand, a personal triumph for Prime Minister Narendra Modi that could now ensure his party's near-domination of politics in India.

BJP registered the biggest-ever victory by any political party in Uttar Pradesh since Indira Gandhi led the Congress to 309 seats in 1980. The results routed the Samajwadi Party-Congress alliance, as well as the Bahujan Samaj Party. Bharatiya Janata Party won this election by an overwhelming three-quarter majority of 325 seats, despite not projecting a chief ministerial candidate before the election. As part of its election strategy BJP contested under a collective leadership and capitalised mostly on the political clout and 'brand' of its leader Prime Minister Narendra Modi. After stunning electoral victory in Uttar Pradesh, BJP picked Hindutva mascot Yogi Adityanath as the State's Chief Minister. While the 44-year-old Chief Minister Yogi Adityanath is a Thakur by caste, one of his Deputy Chief Minister Keshav Prasad Maurya is an OBC and the other Deputy Chief Minister Dinesh Sharma is a Brahmin.

BJP chose to focus heavily on Prime Minister Narendra Modi's presence in Uttarakhand, choosing to play down the lack of local leadership. It was actually the Narendra Modi factor that helped BJP win the election. BJP's aggressive strategy really worked wonders and Modi magic did the rest. Five rallies by Prime Minister Narendra Modi mobilised massive support for the BJP which scripted history bagging 56 of the 70 seats. Chief Minister Harish Rawat lost both the seats he contested in these elections. A Congress candidate who lost to BJP said, "The BJP sweep is an affirmative vote for Prime Minister Narendra Modi." He added that the Congress party needs to do introspection as people "clearly did not accept our agenda and instead voted in the name of Modi." Senior BJP leader 56-year-old Trivendra Singh Rawat, who has a long RSS background, was sworn in as the Uttarakhand Chief Minister.

Appendix 1

Speech of Prime Minister Narendra Modi on 15th August 2014

My dear countrymen,

Today, all Indians in the country and also abroad are celebrating the festival of independence. On this day of sacred festival of independence, the prime servant of India extends greetings to all dear countrymen.

I am present amidst you not as the Prime Minister, but as the Prime Servant. The freedom struggle was fought for so many years, so many generations laid down their lives, innumerable people sacrificed their lives and youth, spent their entire lives behind bars. Today, I pay my respect, greetings and homage to all those who laid their lives for the country's independence.

I also pay my respects to the crores of citizens of this country on the pious occasion of India's independence, and recall all those martyrs who had laid down their lives in India's struggle for freedom. The day of independence is a festival when we take a solemn pledge of working for the welfare of mother India, and also for the welfare of the poor, oppressed, dalits, the exploited & the backward people of our country.

My dear countrymen, a national festival is an occasion to refine and rebuild the national character. This National festival inspires us to resolve ourselves to lead a life where our character gets refined further, to dedicate ourselves to the nation and our every activity is linked to the interest of the nation and only then this festival of freedom can be a festival of inspiration to take India to newer heights.

My dear countrymen, this nation has neither been built by political leaders nor by rulers nor by governments. This nation has been built by our farmers, our workers, our mothers and sisters, our youth. The country has reached here today because of generation to generation rigours undertaken by our sages, our saints, our maestros, our teachers, our scientists and social workers. These great people and these great generations, who had worked for the country throughout their lives, deserve our deepest respect. This is the beauty of India's Constitution, this is its capability which has made it possible that today a boy from small town, a poor family has got the opportunity to pay homage to the tri-colour of India at the ramparts of Lal Qila (Red Fort). This is the strength of India's democracy. This is an invaluable legacy which we have inherited from our architects of the constitution. I pay my respects to those architects of the constitution of India today.

Brothers and sisters, today if we have reached here after independence, it is because of the contribution of all the Prime Ministers, all the governments and even the governments of all the States. I want to express my feelings of respect and gratitude to all those previous governments and ex-Prime

Ministers who have endeavoured to take our present day India to such heights and who have added to the country's glory.

This country has been built on such foundation of ancient cultural heritage, where we were told of only one mantra during Vedic period, which is indicative of our work culture, which we have learnt, we have memorized – *"Sangachchhdhvam Samvadadhvam sam wo manansi jaanataam"* (we walk together, we move together, we think together, we resolve together and together we take this country forward). Having imbibed this basic mantra, 125 crores of countrymen have taken the nation forward. Yesterday only the first Parliamentary Session of the new Government had concluded. Today, I can proudly say that the Session of Parliament reflects our thinking and it is a reflection of our intentions. We are not for moving forward on the basis of majority, we are not interested to move forward by virtue of majority. We want to move ahead on the basis of strong consensus, *'Sangachhadhwam'* and, therefore, the nation has witnessed the entire Session of Parliament. Having taken all the Parties and Opposition along while working shoulder to shoulder, we achieved an unprecedented success and the credit for this does not go to the Prime Minister alone, the credit does not go to the people sitting in the Government, the credit for this goes to the Opposition also, the credit goes to all the leaders of Opposition too and also all the Members from Opposition. From the ramparts of Red Fort, quite proudly I salute all the Members of Parliament, I also salute all the Political Parties and by virtue of their strong support, we could take some important decisions intended to take the nation forward and yesterday the Session of Parliament had concluded.

Brothers and sisters, I am an outsider for Delhi, I am not a native of Delhi. I have no idea about the administration and working of this place. I have been quite isolated from the elite class of this place but during the last two months while being an outsider, I had an insider view and I was astonished. It is not a political platform, rather it is a platform of a national policy and, therefore, my views should not be evaluated from a political perspective. I have already said, I salute all the ex-Prime Ministers and earlier governments who have brought the country thus far. But I am going to say something else and it may not be seen from political point of view. When I came to Delhi and noticed an insider view, I felt what it was and I was surprised to see it. It seemed as if dozens of separate governments are running at the same time in one main government. It appeared that everyone has its own fiefdom. I could observe disunity and conflict among them. One department is taking on the other department and taking on to the extent that two departments of the same government are fighting against each other by approaching Supreme Court. This disunity, this conflict among people of the same country! How come we can take the country forward? And that is why I have started making efforts for razing those walls; I have started making efforts at making the Government, not an assembled entity, but an organic unity, an organic entity, a harmonious whole- with one aim, one mind, one direction, one energy. Let's resolve to steer the country to one destination. We have it in us to move in that direction. A few days back.... Nowadays newspapers are full of news that Modiji's Government has come, officers are reaching office on time, offices open in time, and people get there in time. I observed that India's National newspapers, TV media were carrying these news items prominently. As the Head of the Government I could have derived pleasure in the fact that everything started going on time, cleanliness got the attention, but I was not taking pleasure, I was feeling pained. That thing, I want to tell today in public. And why, because if government officers arrive office in time, does that make a news? And if that makes news, it shows how low we have fallen. It becomes a proof of that, and that's how, brothers and sisters, the governments have run? Today in the face of global competition, when we have to realize the dreams of millions of Indians, the country cannot run on the lines of 'it happens', 'it goes'. In order to fulfil the aspirations of masses, we have to sharpen the tool called the Government machinery, we have to make it keen, more dynamic, and it is in this direction that we are working.

My countrymen, it's not long since I have come from outside Delhi, but I give you an assurance that the people in the Government are very capable – from the peon to the Cabinet Secretary, everybody is capable, everybody has a power, they have experience. I want to awaken that power, I want to unite that power and want to accelerate the pace of the welfare of nation through that power and I shall definitely do it. I want to assure the countrymen that we will achieve that, we will definitely do that. I could not say this on 16th May, but today after my experience of two-two and half months, keeping the tricolour as witness, I am saying on 15th of August that it is possible, it will be achieved.

Brothers and sisters, time has come to give a serious thought to the fact that whether we have a duty to create India of the dreams of those great people who gave us freedom, whether we have a national character? Brothers and sisters, can someone please tell me as to whether he or she has ever introspected in the evening after a full day's work as to whether his or her acts have helped the poor of the country or not, whether his or her actions have resulted in safeguarding the interest of the country or not, whether the actions have been directed in country's welfare or not? Whether it should not be the motto of one and a quarter billion countrymen that every step in life should be in the country's interests? Unfortunately, we have an environment today wherein if you approach anyone with some work, he begins by saying "what does it mean for me?" He begins by saying "what does it involve for me?" and when he come to know that it does not entail any benefit for him, immediately he says "why should I bother?" we have to rise above the feelings of "what does it mean for me" and "why should I bother". Everything is not for self interest only. There are certain things which are meant for the country and we have to refine this national character. We have to rise above the feelings of "why should I bother" and "what does it mean for me" and instead we have to think that "I am for nation's interest and in this field, I am going to lead". We have to inculcate this sentiment.

Brothers and sisters, when we hear about the incidents of rape, we hang our heads in shame. People come out with different arguments, someone indulges in psycho analysis, but brothers and sisters, today from this platform, I want to ask those parents, I want to ask every parent that you have a daughter of 10 or 12 years age, you are always on the alert, every now and then you keep on asking where are you going, when would you come back, inform immediately after you reach. Parents ask their daughters hundreds of questions, but have any parents ever dared to ask their son as to where he is going, why he is going out, who his friends are. After all, a rapist is also somebody's son. He also has parents. As parents, have we ever asked our son as to what he is doing and where he is going. If every parent decides to impose as many restrictions on the sons as have been imposed on our daughters, try to do this with your sons, try to ask such questions of them.

\My dear brothers and sisters, the law will take its own course, strict action will be taken, but as a member of the society, as parents, we also have some responsibilities. If somebody tells me that those who have taken guns on their shoulders and kill innocent people are Maoists, are terrorists, but they are also somebody's children. I would like to ask of such parents if they had ever asked their children as to why they were taking a wrong path. Every parent must take this responsibility, he must know that his misguided son is bent on killing innocent people. He is not able to serve himself nor his family nor the country. I want to say to those youngsters who have chosen the path of violence that whatever they are and wherever they are, it is all because of mother India only that they have got it. Whoever you are it is all because of your parents. I want to ask you to think how green, how beautiful and how beneficial this earth can become if you shoulder the plough instead of the gun which spills blood on this land. How long shall we have bloodshed on this land, how long shall we take the lives of the innocent people and what have we got after all this? The path of violence has not yielded anything to us.

Brothers and sisters, I had gone to Nepal recently. There I said something publicly to draw the attention of the whole world. There was a time when the Emperor Ashoka who had chosen the path of wars, got converted to the path of Buddha at the sight of violence. There was a time in Nepal when their youngsters had opted for the path of violence but today I witness that the same youngsters are waiting for their constitution. The same people associated with them are framing the constitution. And I further said that if Nepal could present the best example of moving from the weapons to the books then it could provide inspiration to the youngsters in the world to abandon the path of violence.

Brothers and sisters, If Nepal, land of Buddha, can give message to the world then why can't India too do the same? So it's the call of the hour that we renounce the path of violence and take the path of brotherhood.

Brothers and sisters, for one reason or the other, we have had communal tensions for ages. This led to the division of the country. Even after Independence, we have had to face the poison of casteism and communalism. How long these evils will continue? Whom does it benefit? We have had enough of fights, many have been killed. Friends, look behind and you will find that nobody has benefited from it. Except casting a slur on Mother India, we have done nothing. Therefore, I appeal to all those people that whether it is the poison of casteism, communalism, regionalism, discrimination on social and economic basis, all these are obstacles in our way forward. Let's resolve for once in our hearts, let's put a moratorium on all such activities for ten years, we shall march ahead to a society which will be free from all such tensions. And you will see that how much strength we get from peace, unity, goodwill and brotherhood. Let's experiment it for once.

My dear countrymen, believe in my words, I do assure you. Shun all the sins committed so far, give up that way, follow the way of goodwill and brotherhood, and let's resolve to take the country forward. I believe we can do that.

With advancement of science, brothers and sisters, we have a rising feeling of modernity in our mind, but what do we do? Have we ever thought what the sex ratio in the country is like? 940 girls are born against per thousand boys. Who is causing this imbalance in the society? Certainly not God. I request the doctors not to kill the girl growing in the womb of a mother just to line their own pockets. I advise mothers and sisters not to sacrifice daughters in the hope of son. Sometimes mother-father feel tempted to have son in the hope of supporting them in old age. I am a person who has worked in public life. I have come across families with five sons, each having bungalows, access to fleet of cars, but parents are forced to live in old-age homes, Vriddhashrams. I have seen such families. I have also seen families with only daughter as progeny, that daughter sacrifices her dreams, doesn't get married, and spends entire life in taking care of old parents. This disparity points to female foeticide and the polluted and tainted mind the 21st century has. We will have to liberate from it, and that is message to us of this Freedom festival.

Recently Commonwealth Games were organized. Indian sportspersons brought glory to the country. Nearly 64 of our sportspersons won. Our sportspersons brought 64 medals. But of them 29 are girls. Let's feel proud and clap for them. Girls also contribute to India's fame and glory. Let's recognise it. Let's take them along, shoulder to shoulder. This way we can get over the evils that have crept in social life. Therefore, brothers and sisters, we have to proceed in that direction as a social and national character. Brothers. and Sisters, Development is the only way forward for the country. Good governance is the only way. There are only these two tracks to take the country forward – good governance and development, we can move forward only by taking them with us. We wish to move forward with the intent of taking them with us. When I talk of good governance, you tell me, when I ask a person in private job, he tells that he does the job; when you ask the same from a person in government job, he says that I do the service. Both earn, but for one it is job while for the other it is service. I ask a question from all brothers and sisters in government service, whether the word "Service" has not lost its strength, its identity? Persons in government service are not doing "job", they are doing "service". We have to revive this feeling, we have to take this feeling forward as a national character, we have to move forward in this direction.

Brothers and Sisters, whether the citizens of the country should take steps for the welfare of the nation or not? You imagine, if this 125 crores of countrymen move one step forward, then the country moves 125 crore steps forward. The meaning of democracy is not just limited to electing a government, but its meaning is that 125 crore of citizens work together joining shoulder with the government to fulfil hopes and aspirations of the country, this is the meaning of democracy. We have to create partnership with the people. We have to proceed under Public-Private Partnership. We have to proceed along with the participation of the people. But, please tell me why our farmers commit suicide? A farmer takes loan from the moneylender, but fails to repay his loans. He takes loan for the wedding of his daughter, but fails to repay. He will have to suffer hardships during his whole life. He chooses to commit suicide. Who will save the poor families of such farmers?

Brothers and sisters, I have come here with a pledge to launch a scheme on this festival of Freedom. It will be called 'Pradhan Mantri Jan-Dhan Yojana'. I wish to connect the poorest citizens of the country with the facility of bank accounts through this Yojana. There are millions of families who have mobile phones but no bank accounts. We have to change this scenario. Economic resources of the country should be utilized for the well-being of the poor. The change will commence from this point. This Yojana will open the window. Therefore, an account holder under 'Pradhan Mantri Jan-Dhan Yojana' will be given a debit card. An insurance of one lakh rupees will be guaranteed with that debit card for each poor family, so that such families are covered with the insurance of one lakh rupees in case of any crisis in their lives.

My brothers and sisters, it is a country of young people. The 65 percent population of the country happens to be under the age of 35 years. Our country has the largest number of youths in the world. Have we ever thought of deriving an advantage out of it? Today, the world needs a skilled workforce. Today, India also needs a skilled workforce. At times, we look for a good driver but he is not available, we look for a plumber, but he is not available. If we need a good cook, he is not available. We have young people, they are unemployed but the kind of young people we seek for are not available. If we have to promote the development of our country then our mission has to be 'skill development' and 'skilled India'. Millions and Millions of Indian youth should go for acquisition of skills and there should be a network across the country for this and not the archaic systems. They should acquire the skills which could contribute towards making India a modern country. Whenever they go to any country in the world, their skills must be appreciated and we want to go for a two pronged development. I also want to create a pool of young people who are able to create jobs and the ones who are not capable of creating jobs and do not have the opportunities, they must be in a position to face their counterparts in any corner of the world while keeping their heads high by virtue of their hard work and their dexterity of hands and win the hearts of people around the world through their skills. We want to go for the capacity building of such young people. My brothers and sisters, having taken a resolve to enhance the skill development at a highly rapid pace, I want to accomplish this.

Brothers and sisters, the world has undergone a change. My dear countrymen, the world has changed. Now India can not decide its future by remaining isolated and sitting alone in a corner. The economics of the world have changed and, therefore, we will have to act accordingly. Government have taken many decisions recently, made some announcements in the budget and I call upon the world and call upon the Indians spread world over that if we have to provide more and more employment to the youth, we will have to promote manufacturing sector. If we have to develop a balance between imports and exports, we will have to strengthen manufacturing sector. If we have to put in use the education, the capability of the youth, we will have to go for manufacturing sector and for this Hindustan also will have to lend its full strength, but we also invite world powers. Therefore I want to appeal all the people world over, from the ramparts of the Red Fort, "Come, make in India", "Come, manufacture in India". Sell in any country of the world but manufacture here. We have got skill, talent, discipline, and determination to do something. We want to give the world an favourable opportunity that come here, "Come, Make in India" and we will say to the world, from electrical to electronics, "Come, Make in India", from automobiles to agro value addition "Come, Make in India", paper or plastic, "Come, Make in India", satellite or submarine "Come, Make in India". Our country is powerful. Come, I am giving you an invitation.

Brothers and sisters, I want to call upon the youth of the country, particularly the small people engaged in the industrial sector. I want to call upon the youth working in the field of technical education in the country. As I say to the world "Come, Make in India", I say to the youth of the country – it should be our dream that this message reaches every corner of the world, "Made in India". This should be our dream. Whether, to serve the country, is it necessary for the youth of the country to be hanged like Bhagat Singh? Brothers and sisters, Lal Bahadur Shastri had given the slogan "Jai Jawan, Jai Kisan". A soldier sacrifices himself at the border and protects Mother India. Similarly, a farmer serves Mother India by filling the godowns with grains. This is also nation's service. Filling the granary is the biggest nation's service that a farmer provides. That is why Lal Bahadur Shastri had given the slogan of "Jai Jawan, Jai Kisan".

Brothers and Sisters, I would like to pose a question to my youngsters as to why despite them, we are forced to import even the smallest of things? My country's youth can resolve it, they should conduct research, try to find out as to what type of items are imported by India and then each one should resolve that, through may be micro or small industries only, he would manufacture at least one such item so that we need not import the same in future. We should even advance to a situation wherein we are able to export such items. If each one of our millions of youngsters resolves to manufacture at least one such item, India can become a net exporter of goods. I, therefore, urge upon the youth, in particular our small entrepreneurs that they would never compromise, at least on two counts. First, zero defect and, second again zero effect. We should manufacture goods in such a way that they carry zero defect, that our exported goods are never returned to us. We should manufacture goods with zero effect that they should not have a negative impact on the environment. If we march ahead with the dream of zero defect in the manufacturing sector then, my brothers and sisters, I am confident that we would be able to achieve our goals.

Brothers and sisters, the youth of India has completely transformed the identity of India in the world. Earlier, in what manner did the world know our country? Till only 25-30 years back, if not more, there were many people in the world who thought that India was a country of snake charmers, it was a country which practised in black magic. The real identity of India had not reached the world, but my dear brothers and sisters, our youngsters, 20-22-23 years old youngsters have mesmerized the whole world with their skills in computers. Our young IT professionals have given a new path of making a new identity of India. If our country has this strength, can we think something about the country? Our dream is, therefore, of "Digital India". When I talk of "Digital India", I don't speak of the elite, it is for the poor people. You can imagine what a quality education the children in villages will get, if all the villages of India are connected with Broadband Connectivity and if we are able to give long distance education to the schools in every remote corner of the villages. If we create a network of telemedicine in the places where there is a shortage of doctors, we can have a clear guideline of the way in which health facilities have to be provided to the poor people living in those areas. The citizens of India have mobile phones in their hands, they have mobile connectivity, but can we walk in the direction of mobile governance? We have to move in a direction where every poor person is able to operate his bank account from his mobile, is able to demand various things from the government, can submit applications, can conduct all his business, while on the move, through mobile governance and if this has to be done, we have to move towards 'digital India' and if we have to move towards 'digital India' then we have a dream. Today we are importing electronic goods on a large scale. Friends, you will be surprised that we are bringing in these televisions, mobile phones, i-pads and all these electronic goods. It is a necessity to import petroleum products, oil, diesel and petrol. Second to this is the import of our electronic goods. If we move ahead with the dream of 'digital India' to manufacture electronic goods and become self reliant at least there, how big can be the benefit for the treasury! Therefore, e-governance is what we need to take this idea of 'digital India' forward. E-governance is easy governance, effective governance and also economic governance. E-governance paves the way for good governance.

There was a time when we used to say that the railways provided connectivity to the country. That was it. I say that today it is IT that has the potential to connect each and every citizen of the country and that is why we want to realise the mantra of unity with the help of 'digital India'.

Brothers and sisters, if we move ahead with all this then I believe that a 'digital India' will have the potential to stand with the world on equal footing. Our youth have that capability, it is an opportunity for them.

Brothers and sisters, we want to promote tourism. Tourism provides employment to the poorest of the poor. Gram seller earns something, auto-rickshaw driver earns something, *pakoda* seller earns something and tea seller also earns something. When there is talk of tea seller, I feel a sense of belongingness. Tourism provide employment to the poorest of the poor. But there is a big obstacle in promoting tourism and in our national character and that is – the filthiness all around us. Whether after independence, after so many years of independence, when we stand at the threshold of one and half decade of 21st century, we still want to live in filthiness? The first work I started here after formation of Government is of cleanliness. People wondered whether it is a work of a Prime Minister? People may feel that it is a trivial work for a Prime Minister but for me this a big work. Cleanliness is very big work. Whether our country can not be clean? If one hundred and twenty five crore countrymen decide that they will never spread filthiness, which power in the world has ability to spread filthiness in our cities and villages? Can't we resolve this much?

Brothers and sisters it will be 150th birth anniversary of Mahatma Gandhi in 2019. How do we celebrate 150th birth anniversary of Mahatma Gandhi? Mahatma Gandhi, who gave us freedom, who brought so much honour to such a big country in the world, what do we give to Mahatma Gandhi? Brothers and Sisters, Mahatma Gandhi had cleanliness and sanitation closest to his heart. Whether we resolve not to leave a speck of dirt in our village, city, street, area, school, temple, hospital, and what have you, by 2019 when we celebrate 150th anniversary of Mahatma Gandhi? This happens not just with the Government, but with public participation. That's why we have to do it together.

Brother and Sisters, we are living in 21st century. Has it ever pained us that our mothers and sisters have to defecate in open? Whether dignity of women is not our collective responsibility? The poor womenfolk of the village wait for the night; until darkness descends, they can't go out to defecate. What bodily torture they must be feeling, how many diseases that act might engender. Can't we just make arrangements for toilets for the dignity of our mothers and sisters? Brothers and Sisters, somebody might feel that a big festival like 15th August is an occasion to talk big. Brothers and Sisters, talking big has its importance, making announcements too has importance, but sometimes announcements raise hopes and when the hopes are not fulfilled, the society sinks into a state of despondency. That's why are in favour of telling those things, which we can fulfil just within our sight. Brothers and sisters, you must be getting shocked to hear the Prime Minister speaking of cleanliness and the need to build toilets from the ramparts of the Red Fort.

Brothers and sisters, I do not know how my speech is going to be criticised and how will people take it. But this is my heartfelt conviction. I come from a poor family, I have seen poverty. The poor need respect and it begins with cleanliness. I, therefore, have to launch a 'clean India' campaign from 2nd October this year and carry it forward in 4 years. I want to make a beginning today itself and that is – all schools in the country should have toilets with separate toilets for girls. Only then our daughters will not be compelled to leave schools midway. Our parliamentarians utilizing MPLAD fund are there. I appeal to them to spend it for constructing toilets in schools for a year. The government should utilise its budget on providing toilets. I call upon the corporate sector also to give priority to the provision of toilets in schools with your expenditure under Corporate Social Responsibility. This target should be finished within one year with the help of state governments and on the next 15th August, we should be in a firm position to announce that there is no school in India without separate toilets for boys and girls.

Brothers and sisters, if we proceed with the dreams, we are in a position to realise them. Today, I wish to tell one more specific thing. It has its own importance to discuss the matters and express the views of nation's interest. However, our Members of Parliament do not get opportunity though they are willing to do something. They can express themselves, write to the government, agitate, give memoranda. Still they do not get opportunity to do something on their own. Today I have come to you with a new idea. We are running so many schemes in the name of the Prime Minister in our country, there are numerous schemes in the name of various leaders. However, today I am going to announce a scheme on behalf of the Member of Parliament – 'Sansad Aadarsh Gram Yojana'. We shall fix some parameters. I urge upon the Members of Parliament to select any one of the villages having population of three to five thousand in your constituency. The parameters will be according to the time, space and situation of that locality. It will include the conditions of health, cleanliness, atmosphere, greenery, cordiality etc. On the basis of those parameters, each of our MPs should make one village of his or her constituency a Model Village by 2016. Can't we do at least this? Shouldn't we do this? If we have to build a nation, we should start from the village. Make a Model Village. The reason of fixing this target for 2016 is that it is a new scheme. It takes time to formulate a scheme and then to implement it. After 2016, select two more villages for this purpose, before we go for the General Elections in 2019. And after 2019, each Member of Parliament, during his/her tenure of 5 years must establish at-least five model villages in his/her area. I also call upon the Members of Parliament from urban areas to adopt one village of their choice. I also urge upon the Members of Parliament from Rajya Sabha to adopt one of the villages. If we provide one model village in each district of India then the surrounding villages shall be automatically inspired to follow that model. Let us establish a model village, let us establish a village well equipped with all systems and facilities. The birth anniversary of Jayaprakash Narayanji happens to be on 11th October. On 11th October, the occasion of birth anniversary of Jayaprakash Narayanji, I will present a complete blueprint of "Sansad Adarsh Gram Yojana" (Members of Parliament Model Village Scheme) before all Members of Parliament and State Governments, and I urge upon State Governments also that as per the feasibility in their respective states, all the Members of Legislative Assembly resolve to establish a model village. You can imagine all the Members of Legislative Assembly and all the Members of Parliament in the country establishing a model village. All of a sudden, there would be a model village in each block of India which could inspire us to transform the amenities in rural areas and could give us a new direction and, therefore, we want to move ahead under this "Sansad Adarsh Gram Yojana".

My dear brothers and sisters, ever since our government has taken charge, there has been a discussion in the newspapers, on TV channels as to what would happen to Planning Commission. I believe that when Planning Commission was constituted, it was done on the basis of the circumstances and the needs of those times. In recent years, Planning Commission has contributed to the growth of the country in its own way. I respect that, I am proud of that, but the prevalent situation in the country is different, global scenario has also changed, governments are no longer the centre of economic activities, the scope of such activities has broadened. State governments have been at the centre of development and I consider this a good indication. If we have to take India forward, it can happen only by taking the states forward. India's federal structure is more important today than in the last 60 years. To strengthen our federal structure, to make our federal structure vibrant, to take our federal structure as a heritage of development, a team of Chief Minister and Prime Minister should be there, a joint team of the Centre and the states should move forward, then to do this job, we will have to think about giving the Planning Commission a look. So, I am saying from the rampart of the Red Fort that it is a very old system and it will have to be rejuvenated, it will have to be changed a lot. Sometimes it costs more to repair the old house, but, it gives us no satisfaction. Thereafter, we have a feeling that it would be better to construct a new house altogether and therefore within a short period, we will replace the planning commission with a new institution having a new design and structure, a new body, a new soul, a new thinking, a new direction, a new faith towards forging a new direction to lead the country based on creative thinking, public-private partnership, optimum utilization of resources, utilization of youth power of the nation, to promote the aspirations of state governments seeking development, to empower the state governments and to empower the federal structure. Very shortly, we are about to move in a direction when this institute would be functioning in place of Planning Commission.

Brothers and sisters, today, on 15th August, we also have the birth anniversary of Maharishi Aurobindo. Maharishi Aurobindo, being a rebel, moved on to achieve the status of a Yoga Guru. With regard to the destiny of India, he remarked, "I have a faith that the divine power and spiritual heritage of India will play an important role towards the welfare of the world." Such sentiments were echoed by Maharishi Arvind. I strongly believe in the words of legends. I have great faith in the statements made by ascetics, sages & saints and that's why today at the ramparts of Lal Qila I am reminded of the words of Swami Vivekananda. He had said – "I can see before my eyes Mother India awakening once again. My Mother India would be seated as the World Guru. Every Indian would render service towards welfare of humanity. This legacy of India would be useful for the welfare of the world". These words were spoken by Swami Vivekanandaji in his own style. Friends, the words of Vivekanandaji can never be untrue. The words of Vivekanandaji, his dream of seeing India ensconced as World Guru, his vision, it is incumbent upon us to realize that dream. This capable country, blessed with natural bounty, this country of youth can do much for the world in the coming days.

Brothers and sisters, our foreign policy is a much talked about issue. I clearly believe that India's foreign policy can be multi-dimensional. But there is an important issue to which I want to draw your attention that the way we fought for freedom, we fought together, we were not separate at that time. We were together. Which was the government with us? What were the weapons available to us? There was a Gandhi, a Sardar and lakhs of freedom fighters and such a huge empire. Didn't we win in the struggle of freedom against that empire? Did we not defeat the foreign powers? Did we not force them to leave India? We were the ones, they were our ancestors only who showed this might. If the people of India could remove such a big empire without the power of the government, without weapons and even without resources, then friends, it is the need of the hour to eradicate poverty, can we not overcome poverty? Can we not defeat poverty? My 125 crore dear countrymen, let us resolve to eradicate poverty, to win against it. Let us move with the dream of poverty eradication from India. Our neighbouring countries are also faced with the same problem. Why not get together with all the SAARC nations to plan out the fight against poverty? Let's fight together and defeat poverty. Let us see at-least for once as to how wonderful is the feeling of being alive instead of killing and getting killed. This is the land where incidents from

Siddharth's life happened. One bird was shot with an arrow by one brother and the other took out that arrow to save it. They went to mother- whose bird, whose swan? Whether killer's or saviour's, they asked of mother. The mother replied, saviour's. The saviour has more power than the killer and that makes him Buddha in future. And that's why I seek cooperation from neighbouring countries for fighting against poverty in concert and cooperate with them, so that together with SAARC countries we can create our importance and emerge as a power in the world. It is imperative that we work together with a dream to win a fight against poverty, shoulder to shoulder. I went to Bhutan, Nepal, all the dignitaries from SAARC countries took part in oath-taking ceremony; this marked a good beginning. This will definitely yield good results, it is my belief and this thinking of India, in the country and the world, that we want to do well to the countrymen and be useful for the welfare of the world, India wants such a hand to be extended. We are trying to move forward with these dreams to achieve them.

Brothers and Sisters, today on 15th August we will resolve to do something for the country. Let's be useful for the country, we will move ahead with a resolve to take the country forward, and I assure you, Brothers and Sisters, as well as my colleagues in the Government, that if you work for 12 hours, I will do so for 13 hours. If you work for 14 hours, I will do for 15 hours. Why? Because I'm amidst you not as a Prime Minister, but as the first servant. I have formed the Government not as a ruler, but as a servant. Brothers and sisters, I assure that this country has a destiny. It is destined to work for the welfare of the world, it was said by Vivekanandji. India is born, this

Hindustan is born in order to achieve this destiny. One hundred and twenty five crore countrymen have to move forward wholeheartedly for the welfare of the nation.

Once again I feel proud of the devotion, the sacrifices of the security forces of the country, para-military forces of the country, all the security forces of the country to protect Mother India. I say to the countrymen, "Eternal vigilance is the price of liberty". The army is vigilant, we should also be vigilant and the country scales new heights, we have to move forward with this resolution. Speak loudly with me with full force –

Bharat mata ki jai, bharat mata ki jai, bharat mata ki jai.

Jai Hind, Jai Hind, Jai Hind.

Vande Mataram, Vande Mataram, Vande Mataram!

Appendix 2

Pro-Poor Welfare Schemes Launched by Prime Minister Narendra Modi

The Central Government under the leadership of Prime Minister Narendra Modi launched following welfare schemes for the development of poor and farmers throughout the country within a short span of time.

PRADHAN MANTRI JAN DHAN YOJANA (PMJDY)

Pradhan Mantri Jan Dhan Yojana (PMJDY) was launched by Prime Minister Narendra Modi on 28th August 2014 at national level. The accounts that can be opened under PMJDY are Basic Savings Bank Deposit Accounts (BSBDA) which can be with zero balance as per Reserve Bank of India guidelines. 28.23 crore accounts opened so far. Deposits in these accounts have now exceeded ₹63,971.38 crore.

MAKE IN INDIA

Make in India is an initiative launched by Prime Minister Narendra Modi on 25 September 2014 to encourage multinational, as well as national companies to manufacture their products in India. India emerged, after initiation of the programme in 2015, as the top destination globally for foreign direct investment (FDI), surpassing the United States of America as well as the People's Republic of China. The major objective behind the initiative is to focus on job creation and skill enhancement in 25 sectors of the economy. The initiative also aims at high quality standards and minimising the impact on the environment. The initiative hopes to attract capital and technological investment in India. Under the initiative, brochures on the 25 sectors and a web portal were released. Before the initiative was launched, foreign equity caps in various sectors had been relaxed. The application for licenses was made available online and the validity of licenses was increased to three years. Various other norms and procedures were also relaxed. In August 2014, Government of India allowed 49 per cent foreign direct investment (FDI) in the defence sector and 100 per cent in railways infrastructure. The defence sector previously allowed 26 per cent FDI and FDI was not allowed in railways. This was in hope of bringing down the military imports of India. Earlier, one Indian company would have held the 51 per cent stake, this was changed so that multiple companies could hold the 51 per cent. Between September 2014 and November 2015, the government received ₹1.20 lakh crore worth of proposals from companies interested in manufacturing electronics in India. 24.8 per cent of smartphones shipped in the country in the April-June quarter of 2015 were made in India, up from 19.9 per cent the previous quarter.

SWACHH BHARAT ABHIYAN

Swachh Bharat Abhiyan (Clean India Movement) is a campaign, launched on 2 October 2014 by Prime Minister Narendra Modi, to clean the streets, roads and infrastructure of the country's 4,041 cities and towns. It is India's largest ever cleanliness drive with 30 lakh government employees, and especially school and college students from all parts of India, participating in the campaign. The objectives of Swachh Bharat are to reduce or eliminate open defecation through construction of individual, cluster and community toilets. The Swachh Bharat Abhiyan will also make an initiative of establishing an accountable mechanism of monitoring latrine use. Modi government is aiming to achieve an Open-Defecation Free (ODF) India by 2 October 2019, the 150th anniversary of the birth of Mahatma Gandhi, by constructing 1.2 crore toilets in rural India, at a projected cost of ₹1.96 lakh crore. Swachh Bharat Mission (Gramin) since 2nd October 2014: 3,89,43,140 household toilets built, 1,89,501 open defecation free villages, 3,741 open defecation free villages in Namami Gange, 130 open defecation free districts. Swachh Bharat Mission (Urban) since 2nd October 2014: construction achieved of 31,14,249 individual toilets, construction achieved of 1,15,786 community and public toilets, number of open defecation free cities: 588.

SUKANYA SAMRIDDHI YOJANA (SSY)

Sukanya Samriddhi Yojana was launched by Prime Minister Narendra Modi on 21st January 2015; under the Beti Bachao, Beti Padhao campaign. This scheme was launched to meet the expenses of the girl child's higher education and marriage. An SSY account can only be opened in the name of a girl child (beneficiary) below 10 years, as on the date of the opening of the account. The rules allow for the opening of a maximum of two accounts for two girls in a family. One can't open two accounts for one girl. When the beneficiary, i e, the girl child crosses the age of 10, she can operate the account on her own. To open an SSY account, a minimum initial deposit of ₹1,000 is required. Thereafter, a minimum of ₹1,000 up to a maximum of ₹1.5 lakh can be deposited in the account annually. To keep the account active, deposits need to be made only for the initial 15 years. For a 9-year-old, deposits have to continue till the child turns 24. Between ages 24 and 30 (when the account matures), the account keeps earning interest on the balance. It is currently (2016-17) fetching an interest rate of 9.1 per cent and provides income-tax rebate.

PRADHAN MANTRI MUDRA YOJANA (PMMY)

Pradhan Mantri MUDRA Yojana (PMMY) was launched by Prime Minister Narendra Modi on 8th April 2015 to help the needy. The aim of this scheme is to provide financial assistance (by providing loans at reasonable interest rates). Depending on the size of business loans are being offered accordingly. Under this scheme, loans up to ₹10 lakh are being provided. The MUDRA loans have been classified as – Shishu Loan, Kishore Loan and Tarun Loan. All non-farming micro business that generate income and are in need of monetary aid below or up to ₹10 lakh can apply for this loan under the Pradhan Mantri MUDRA Yojana. Pradhan Mantri MUDRA Bank already has a corpus of more than ₹70,000 crore and this amount would help in increasing the overall output and creating newer jobs. MUDRA Bank Loan Yojana comes as a vision from the Prime Minister Narendra Modi by the slogan, 'Fund the Unfunded'. MUDRA means Micro Units Development and Refinance Agency.

PRADHAN MANTRI JEEVAN JYOTI BIMA YOJANA (PMJJBY)

Pradhan Mantri Jeevan Jyoti Bima Yojana (PMJJBY) was launched by Prime Minister Narendra Modi on 9th May 2015. PMJJBY is available to people between 18 and 50 years of age with bank accounts. It has an annual premium of ₹330. The amount will be automatically debited from the account. In case of death due to any cause, the payment to the nominee will be ₹2 lakh. This scheme will be linked to the bank accounts opened under the Pradhan Mantri Jan Dhan Yojana scheme. 3.10 crore Jeevan Jyoti Bima policies so far.

PRADHAN MANTRI SURAKSHA BIMA YOJANA (PMSBY)

Pradhan Mantri Suraksha Bima Yojana (PMSBY) was launched by Prime Minister Narendra Modi on 9th May 2015. PMSBY is available to people between 18 and 70 years of age with bank accounts. It has an annual premium of ₹12. The amount will be automatically debited from the account. In case of accidental death or full disability, the payment to the nominee will be ₹2 lakh and in case of partial Permanent disability ₹1 lakh. Full disability has been defined as loss of use in both eyes, hands or feet. Partial Permanent disability has been defined as loss of use in one eye, hand or foot. This scheme will be linked to the bank accounts opened under the

Pradhan Mantri Jan Dhan Yojana scheme. 9.93 crore Suraksha Bima policies so far.

ATAL PENSION YOJANA (APY)

Atal Pension Yojana (APY) was launched by Prime Minister Narendra Modi on 9th May 2015. In Atal Pension Yojana, for every contribution made to the pension fund, The Central Government would also co-contribute 50% of the total contribution or ₹1,000 per annum, whichever is lower, to each eligible subscriber account, for a period of 5 years. The minimum age of joining APY is 18 years and maximum age is 40 years. The age of exit and start of pension would be 60 years. Therefore, minimum period of contribution by the subscriber under APY would be 20 years or more. This scheme will be linked to the bank accounts opened under the Pradhan Mantri Jan Dhan Yojana scheme and the contributions will be deducted automatically. If a new subscriber starts contributing at the age of 18, the monthly amount required will be ₹42 every month to receive a pension amount of ₹1,000. Subscribers can choose to get a monthly pension of ₹1,000, ₹2,000, ₹3,000, ₹4,000 and ₹5,000.

PRADHAN MANTRI AWAS YOJANA (PMAY)

Pradhan Mantri Awas Yojana (PMAY) is a mission started with an aim 'Housing For All' was launched by Prime Minister Narendra Modi on 25th June 2015. The primary aim of this Yojana is to ensure that 2 crore houses are built across nation's length and breadth. The estimated completion year for the scheme is 2022, which means that these 2 crore homes will be constructed over a period of 7 years. Housing for All (HFA) scheme is envisioned by Prime Mister Narendra Modi. "By the time the Nation completes 75 years of its Independence, Pradhan Mantri Awas Yojana will bring a 'Pucca house' for every family in urban cities with water connection, toilet facilities, 24×7 electricity supply and complete access." As addressed by our Prime Minister in the joint session of parliament on 9th June, 2014.

PRADHAN MANTRI KAUSHAL VIKAS YOJANA (PMKVY)

Pradhan Mantri Kaushal Vikas Yojana (PMKVY), launched on 16th July 2015 by Prime Minister Narendra Modi, is the flagship scheme of the Ministry of Skill Development and Entrepreneurship (MSDE). The aim of the scheme is to encourage aptitude towards employable skills and to increase working efficiency of probable and existing daily wage earners, by giving monetary awards and rewards and by providing quality training to them. Those wage earners already possessing a standard level of skill will be given recognition as per scheme and average award amount for them is ₹2,000 to ₹2,500. Training programmes have been worked out on the basis of National Occupational Standards (NOS) and qualification packs specifically developed in various sectors of skills. For this qualification plans and quality plans have been developed by various Sector Skill Councils (SSC) created with participation of Industries. National Skill Development Council (NSDC) has been made coordinating and driving agency for the same. An outlay of ₹12,000 crores has been approved by the cabinet for this project. The scheme has a target to train 1 crore Indian youth from 2016-20. The scheme has a target to train 1 crore Indian youth from 2016-20. As of 18 July 2016, 17.93 lakh candidates were trained out of 18 lakh who enrolled for the scheme.

PRADHAN MANTRI FASAL BIMA YOJANA (PMFBY)

Pradhan Mantri Fasal Bima Yojana (PMFBY) was launched by Prime Minister Narendra Modi on 18th February 2016. Crop insurance has been made affordable by the government using Fasal Bima Yojana. It envisages a uniform premium of only 2 per cent to be paid by farmers for Kharif crops, and 1.5 per cent for Rabi crops. The premium for annual commercial and horticultural crops will be 5 per cent. This scheme is dedicated to bring in more than 50% of the farmers under its wing within the next 2-3 years. Around 25% of the claims will be sent to the farmer's direct account. Also, the scheme will remain as it is. This means that there will be no cap on coverage. Also there won't be any cap on the reduction in the insured sum. This insurance scheme, unlike the previous ones, covers local calamities too, such as landslide, hailstorm, inundation, etc. Inundation was not covered by the previous schemes. Government of India announced a budget allocation of ₹13,240 crore for 2017-18 for Fasal Bima Yojana.

PRADHAN MANTRI UJJWALA YOJANA (PMUY)

Pradhan Mantri Ujjwala Yojana (PMUY) is a welfare programme, launched by Prime Minister Narendra Modi on 1st May 2016. Under this scheme, 5 crore LPG connections will be provided to BPL families with a support of ₹1,600 per connection in the next 3 years. Ensuring women's empowerment, especially in rural India, the connections will be issued in the name of women of the households. ₹8,000 crore has been allocated towards the implementation of the scheme. As of 3 April 2017, 2 crore LPG connections had been completed under PMUY scheme. PMUY is likely to result in an additional employment of around 1 lakh and provide business opportunity of at least ₹10,000 crore over the next 3 years to the Indian Industry. Launch of this scheme will also provide a great boost to the 'Make in India' campaign as all the manufacturers of cylinders, gas stoves, regulators, and gas hose are domestic. It is guided by a strong commitment to bring in change in lives of poor women.

PRADHAN MANTRI GARIB KALYAN YOJANA 2016 (PMGKY)

Pradhan Mantri Garib Kalyan Yojana 2016 (PMGKY) is an amnesty scheme launched by Prime Minister Narendra Modi in December 2016 on the lines of the Income declaration scheme, 2016 (IDS) launched earlier in the year. A part of the Taxation Laws (Second Amendment) Act, 2016, the scheme provides an opportunity to declare unaccounted wealth and black money in a confidential manner and avoid prosecution after paying a fine of 50 per cent on the undisclosed income. An additional 25 per cent of the undisclosed income is invested in the scheme which can be refunded after four years, without any interest. Valid from 16th December 2016 to 31st March 2017, the scheme can only be availed to declare income in the form of cash or bank deposits in Indian bank accounts and not in the form of jewellery, stock, immovable property, or deposits in overseas accounts. Not declaring undisclosed income under the PMGKY will attract a fine of 77.25 per cent if the income is shown in tax returns. In case the income is not shown in tax returns, it will attract a further 10 per cent penalty followed by prosecution. The government has managed to garner ₹2,300 crore through its three-month long tax compliance window, PMGKY, which was provided for people to come clean with their unaccounted cash and deposits after demonetisation.

PRADHAN MANTRI KRISHI SINCHAI YOJANA (PMKSY)

Pradhan Mantri Krishi Sinchai Yojana (PMKSY) is a national mission to improve farm productivity and ensure better utilization of the resources in the country. The budget of ₹50,000 crore in a time span of five years has been allocated to this scheme. The decision was taken on 1 July 2015 at the meeting of Cabinet Committee on Economic Affairs (CCEA), which in turn was headed by the Prime Minister, Narendra Modi. The primary objectives of PMKSY are to attract investments in irrigation system at field level, develop and expand cultivable land in the country, enhance ranch water use in order to minimize wastage of water, enhance crop per drop by implementing water-saving technologies and precision irrigation. The plan additionally calls for bringing ministries, offices, organizations, research and financial institutions occupied with creation and recycling of water under one platform so that an exhaustive and holistic outlook of the whole water cycle is considered. The goal is to open the doors for optimal water budgeting in all sectors. Tagline for PMKSY is "more crop per drop". The scheme will be implemented by Ministries of Agriculture, Water Resources and Rural

Development. Ministry of Rural Development is to mainly undertake rain water conservation, construction of farm pond, water harvesting structures, small check dams and contour bunding etc. MoWR, RD&GR, is to undertake various measures for creation of assured irrigation source, construction of diversion canals, field channels, water diversion/lift irrigation, including development of water distribution systems. Ministry of Agriculture will promote efficient water conveyance and precision water application devices like drips, sprinklers, pivots, rain-guns in the farm (*Jal Sinchan*), construction of micro-irrigation structures to supplement source creation activities, extension activities for promotion of scientific moisture conservation and agronomic measures.

BETI BACHAO BETI PADHAO (BPBB)

Prime Minister Narendra Modi launched the Beti Bachao Beti Padhao programme on 22 January 2015. Beti Bachao, Beti Padhao (Save girl child, educate girl child) is a social campaign that aims to generate awareness and improve the efficiency of welfare services meant for girls. The scheme was launched with an initial corpus of ₹100 crore. The Beti Bachao, Beti Padhao (BBBP) scheme was introduced to address the issue of declining child sex ratio (CSR) and related issues of women empowerment over a life-cycle continuum. The key elements of the scheme include Enforcement of PC&PNDT Act, nationwide awareness and advocacy campaign and multi-sectoral action in select 100 districts (low on CSR) in the first phase. There is a strong emphasis on mindset change through training, sensitization, awareness raising and community mobilization on ground. The NDA Government is trying to bring about a transformational shift in the way our society looks at the girl child.

GOLD MONETISATION SCHEME

Gold lying in the locker/home appreciates in value if gold price goes up but it doesn't pay any regular interest or dividend. The monetisation scheme will allow to earn some regular interest on gold. It is a gold savings account which will earn interest for the gold deposited in it. Gold can be deposited in any physical form – jewellery, coins or bars. This gold will then earn interest based on gold weight and also the appreciation of the metal value. You get back your gold in the equivalent of 995 fineness gold or Indian rupees as you desire (the option to be exercised at the time of deposit). The designated banks will accept gold deposits under the Short Term (1-3 years) Bank Deposit as well as Medium (5-7 years) and Long (12-15 years) Term Government Deposit Schemes.

BANKNOTE DEMONETISATION

On 8 November 2016, Prime Minister Narendra Modi announced the demonetisation in an unscheduled live televised address to the nation at 8.15 PM. In the announcement, Prime Minister declared circulation of all ₹500 and ₹1,000 banknotes of the Mahatma Gandhi Series as invalid effective from the midnight of the same day, and announced the issuance of new ₹500 and ₹2,000 banknotes of the Mahatma Gandhi New Series in exchange for the old banknotes. After Prime Minister's announcement, the

Governor of the Reserve Bank of India, Urjit Patel, and Economic Affairs Secretary, Shaktikanta Das explained in a press conference that one purpose of the action was to fight terrorism funded by counterfeit notes. While the supply of notes of all denominations had increased by 40 per cent between 2011 and 2016, the ₹500 and ₹1,000 banknotes increased by 76 per cent and 109 per cent, respectively, owing to forgery. They said that forged cash was used to fund terrorist activities against India and that the demonetisation had a counter-terrorism purpose. Patel also informed that the decision had been made about six months ago, and the printing of new banknotes of denomination ₹500 and ₹2,000 had already started. However, only the top members of the government, security agencies and the central bank were aware of the move.

"You have all seen the public opinion on demonetisation. The traditional vote, which used to connect with you, has refused to accept this policy (of opposing demonetisation)," Finance Minister Arun Jaitley said in the Lok Sabha, in an apparent reference to the recent poll results, particularly in Uttar Pradesh where the BJP got a resounding victory. Hailing the Prime Minister for the demonetisation decision, Jaitley said, "A strong leader takes unpopular decisions, while the other takes decisions looking at his interests. Narendra Modi is a leader who takes decisions in the national interest." "For 10 years, those who controlled the economic management of the country, they explained to you this and you decided your position accordingly and you saw the results," Jaitley told the Congress benches, while taking a dig at former Prime Minister Dr Manmohan Singh. The Congress Party had bitterly attacked the government over demonetisation before the elections as well as during the poll campaigning.

Bihar Chief Minister Nitish Kumar said that there was no need to oppose demonetisation so strongly since the poor were satisfied and they thought the rich and mighty were hurt by the move. He also noted that a lot of parties ignored the ground reality of demonetisation.

Appendix 3

Speech of Prime Minister Atal Bihari Vajpayee on 15th August 1998

Jai Jawan, Jai Kisan, Jai Vigyan

My dear Sisters, Brothers and Children,

I greet all of you on the occasion of the 51st Anniversary of our country's Independence. Half a century has passed still it appears as if it happened yesterday. Pandit Jawaharlal Nehru had unfurled our beloved tricolour in the blue sky from this very spot for the first time. Since then it has been a tradition to unfurl the National flag from the historic Red Fort. I had never imagined that I shall have this good fortune one day. It is a symbol of strength and potential of the Indian democracy that the son of a school teacher hailing from the dusty and smoky environs of a village has the privilege of unfurling the national tricolour from the ramparts of Red Fort on this auspicious Independence Day.

We all know that independence did not come to us easily. On the hand, while tens of thousands of our countrymen and women suffered in jails during the non-violent freedom struggle under the leadership of Mahatma Gandhi, on the other hand, thousands of revolutionaries sacrificed their lives on the gallows. We owe our independence to these known and unknown martyrs and freedom fighter. Let all of us together pay homage to them and take a pledge that we shall defend our freedom, even if we have to sacrifice everything for this.

Our country has been subjected to foreign aggression. In this short period of 50 years, we had to face four aggressions. But we have safeguarded our independence and integrity. The highest credit for this undoubtedly goes to our soldiers. Away from their homes and dear ones, braving dangers all the time, they guard our frontiers day and night. This is why we are always reassured about our security. Be it the snowy expanse of Siachen with minus 32 degree Celsius temperature or the thick forests of the North-East, the deserts of Kutch or Jaisalmer or the deep waters of the Indian Ocean our troops are vigilant everywhere. On our behalf I greet all these troops of the Army, the Air Force and the Navy and other security personnel. While congratulating them we must say "O! Brave Soldiers, we are proud of you!"

The Forces need our support. Our farmers and labour force have strengthened the second line of defence in the farms, the barns and the factories. We can never forget this. Lal Bahadur Shastri had said: Jai Jawan, Jai Kisan One is incomplete without the other, unfulfilled without the other. I have added a new aspect to this Jai Vigyan!

POKHRAN TEST

We can neither develop nor defend the country in the 21st century with the resources of the past century. We have to modernise our forces to enable them to face and danger and safeguard our independence and integrity. With only this aim, we conducted the nuclear tests on the 11th and 13th of May this year. The tests of Pokhran were not the efforts of just one night. They were the results of years of hard work on the part of our scientists, engineers, technicians and the defence forces. I have only tried to further the work the foundation of which was credit by Smt Indira Gandhi. I was only a means. The credit for this great achievement goes to our talented scientists and the hard work of our defence forces. I wish to heartily congratulate all of them on this auspicious occasion of this Independence Day.

I am even grateful to all of you for extending your full support in this trying hour. With a few exceptions every Indian, wherever he may be living, has welcomed this step. Holding our head high that day we proudly proclaimed we are Indians . For that day in Pokhran, the might of the Nation manifested itself along with nuclear energy.

I wish to make it clear right now that India has always been an ardent advocate of peace and will always remain so. We know and want to see weapons for self-defence only. We would never use atomic weapons for attacking anyone. Hence, we have put a self-moratorium on any new nuclear tests. We ourselves proclaimed to the world that we shall never be the first user of atomic weapons. We are doing it neither under pressure nor fear of any one. We are doing it voluntarily because of our firm belief in world peace and disarmament. Our dream is to see the world free from nuclear weapons and we want to see this dream come true. Initially, some countries did not appreciate our national security policy needs and doubted our intention. Some of them imposed economic sanctions against us. But now the situation is changing. The world is gradually appreciating the Indian viewpoint. We have been able to make them understand our position. As a result, some of the sanctions have begun to ease. We welcome this changing global attitude.

However, we also want to make one point clear. India is a great country and its people are powerful. The brave people of our country are always ready to face any danger to defend their honour. Our history bears testimony to this. No force on earth can deflect us from our chosen path. I am saying this not out of arrogance but with humility and self-confidence. We are willing to make any sacrifice to uphold the unity, integrity and sovereignty of our country. We wish to improve relations with our neighbours. We know that the easiest way to win a war is not to let it happen. We are ready to hold talks with Pakistan on any subject, at any level and at any time.

You all know that I have taken the initiative during the SAARC Conference in Colombo. I am somewhat unhappy that we did not get the desired response. Still I have not given up. I will make another effort at reviving the dialogue during the Conference of the Non-Aligned countries in South Africa at the end of this month.

I believe that all problems of the world can be solved through talks. Therefore whether it is Pakistan or China, we will endeavour to solve our mutual problems through friendly talks. In the last few days terrorise activities have increased in Jammu and Kashmir. The massacre in Himachal Pradesh appears to be part of a bigger conspiracy. Such terrorist activities everyday, from across the border, are like a proxy war.

Government has taken these incidents very seriously. We are facing them with all our might and we will not rest content until we have defeated these.

TIME FOR RETROSPECTION

Whether in personal or national life, the 51st anniversary is always a golden opportunity to assess the past fifty years. It is also the time for retrospection and preparation for a leap into the 21st century. While making an assessment we most often commit mistakes, tend to undertake our achievements and magnify our shortcomings which result in gloom.

Sometimes, I see a growing tendency of pessimism in the country. There may have been aberrations here and there but things have not gone that bad so as to defy solutions. Our scriptures say that only fools indulge in self-praise. But unnecessary self-condemnation is also like suicide. I want that a realistic assessment of the last fifty years should be undertaken.

NATIONAL INTEGRATION AND SECULARISM

When we attained Independence, some Western experts had forecast that we were unfit for being a democracy and did not deserve freedom. They said we would soon disintegrate. But, today, we can say with pride that we have not only safeguarded our integrity and independence but have also shown to the world how the biggest democracy can be governed. Almost all the countries which gained freedom along with us have kept the democratic tradition alive. This is our 12th Lok Sabha and I am the 11th Prime Minister of India. We have seen over the years transformations taking place from the tiniest village Panchayat to the Parliament. You all deserve credit for this. Your political maturity in all these elections have baffled political pundits. I congratulate you for this. Our democracy is safe as long as you remain vigilant.

On the occasion of the golden jubilee celebrations of our Independence, the Nation has to address itself to the important fact that Independence, national integration, democracy and secularism are complementary to each other.

We have to remain independent under all circumstances. An essential condition for this is national unity. Democracy is necessary for national unity. Secularism and democracy are inseparable parts of national unity. I and my Government are committed to all these four elements.

We oppose communalism in any form. We will ensure full security of the minorities and guarantee their participation in development. We should never forget that we are the citizens of one country. The boundaries of this country extend from Ladakh to Nicobar, from Garo Hills to Gilgit. Ours is a country whose civilisation and culture is more than five thousand years old. Such a big country replete with varieties of language, faith, living and food habits has resolved to achieve social and economic justice within the framework of democracy. Simultaneously, we cannot forget that we have to strive to rid this democracy of aberrations. Our legislators behave in such a way in legislatures that even a school teacher would not tolerate system of governance through free debate. The opposition has the right to criticise and government has the right to implement. The opposition and the government are complementary to each other and adversaries.

Fearless and impartial voting has to be further strengthened. The electoral system has to be reformed to free it from casteism, violence, money power and other ills so that in the next century our system of governance is further refined.

TITLE OF FOOD PROVIDERS

Once upon a time, this country was a land of prosperity. The situation deteriorated and we began to be counted among the poor nations of the world. In the past few years our farmers and agricultural workers have worked very hard to make the country self-sufficient in foodgrain production. An army with an empty stomach cannot fight and a hungry nation cannot have a restful sleep. Our farmers have made the country self-sufficient to justify their being called Food Providers . I can only pray to God that He shower happiness on the Food Providers .

There is a shadow of sorrow in this happiness. Today the condition of our Food Providers has become difficult. I feel very pained that this year in some states some farmers have had to commit suicide because they could not bear the burden of their debts. I offer my condolences to the bereaved families. As a tribute to these farmers I have taken a decision. The Crop Insurance scheme will be broadened, new crops will be brought within its purview and its geographical reach will be creased.

A high-powered Commission will be formed to look into the real financial condition of farmers and to improve their economic condition. I want to assure our farmer brothers who are the backbones of the Nation that they will never suffer under this Government.

EASY TO SAY, HARD TO ACHIEVE

In Orissa, hunger still stalks the people in places like Balangir, Kalahandi and Koraput. It is unimaginable that even 50 years after independence some people are still stalked by hunger. I have told the Planning Commission that the outlay on the Employment Assurance Scheme in these areas should be doubled. My efforts will be to ensure that no one dies of hunger. The country has made commendable progress in business, industry and services. Some of our industries are making their mark on the international scene. I congratulate all the workers, employees, managers, industrialists and businessmen for this achievement.

But we know that this achievement is only a stepping stone. It is not the attainment of the final goal which is to see the rise of India as an economic superpower. I know that saying this is much easier than doing it. For this, We will need to follow the path of hard work, establish high standards and depend on self-reliance. We will have to produce goods of international standard, which can compete in the global markets. Economic reforms will have to be speeded up. But we will not allow others to take undue advantage of our liberalisation. We will implement infrastructure projects with speed.

Swadeshi does not mean an inward looking policy. The word has become a global village. Each one is dependent on the other. In this open market system we can use our inner strength to stand up to global competition and I have faith that we will.

This 51st Independence Day is being celebrated not only in India but also round the world. Every person of Indian origin in every country is celebrating this sacred occasion with joy and enthusiasm. I give my good wishes to every person of Indian origin round the globe on this occasion. In some countries our brothers and sisters are watching it live on television.

Non-Resident Indians (NRIs) have brought strength to the economies of the nations where they have settled. Now they have an opportunity to strengthen India's economy. We have floated the Resurgent India Bond (RIB). Non-Resident Indians around the world are taking benefit of this opportunity. So far, the scheme has brought in ₹5,000 crore. I am confident that Non-Resident Indians will take further advantage of this scheme.

We will have to solve these problems. I know that all of you, especially our sisters, are feeling the pinch of the rising prices of some commodities. I understand your problem. Nature is to be blamed more for this than the Government. But I know that by saying this your burden will not be lightened. The Finance Ministry and the State Governments will work together to combat the price rise. I also ask for the cooperation of traders. They should not indulge in hoarding or profit- making. We will not hesitate in taking strong measures against such elements. I know that a number of festivals are coming up in the next few days. My efforts will be able to see that rising prices do not dampen your festive spirit.

PROBLEM OF CORRUPTION

The country faces another problem that of corruption which is eating into the vitals of the country like cancer. We have decided to fight it. We have begun the fight from the top. I have not even left out the Prime Minister from the ambit of the Lok Pal Bill, which was recently introduced in the Lok Sabha. This has made clear our intentions to fight corruption at the highest level.

Along with this, we wish to fight corruption in the bureaucracy. Very soon, I will initiate action to speed up work in the cell in the Prime Minister's Office (PMO) which is looking into corruption cases against officials. Removal of unemployment is an important pledge in our National Agenda. It is affecting the lives of everyone. Employment is the only way of fulfilling the basic needs of the people. Creation of schemes for total employment is difficult, but not impossible. But basic needs and services will have to be produced by the masses. Science and technology will have to be applied for this.

Government has decided that ten crore people should get employment opportunities over the next ten years. This means that every year one crore people should get employment opportunities. A task force will be set up for this purpose and it will present its report soon.

RESERVATION FOR WOMEN

The status of women is a good indicator to judge the progress of a modern society. We had promised to give women 33% reservation in Parliament and the Assemblies. We are sorry that we have not been able to fulfil this so far. We have already decided to provide free education to girls up to graduation levels. Now we are going to take another major initiative. All girls at the primary level will be provided books in their curriculum free of cost. This will cost ₹550 crore to the Government.

RAJRAJESHWARI AND BHAGYASHREE YOJANA

A new Insurance Scheme, Rajrajeshwari will be started to provide women the economic security. Another insurance scheme, Bhagyashree will be started for girls. Both schemes will begin on Diwali Day this year. The premium for the scheme will be ₹1 per month. And the policyholder will be able to get ₹25,000 in case of emergency. The full details will be announced soon.

SPEED UP IMPLEMENTATION OF RESERVATION IN JOBS

Reservation in jobs has already been provided to the Scheduled Castes, Scheduled Tribes and Other Backward Classes. However, implementation of these provisions is very slow. My Government's efforts will be to speed up the implementation process and to fill the reservation quotas as quickly as possible. The administration will be made more sensitive and accountable to these classes.

NATIONAL RECONSTRUCTION FORCE

Youth power is the strength of the nation. It is also the future of the nation. Many years ago I had read the words of Baba Amte *"Haath lage nirman mey, nahin mangne, marne"* (use your hands to create, not to ask or hit). This is also our wish. The young girls and boys of India do not have to extend their hands before anyone, nor do they have to use their hands against anyone. They should only dedicate themselves to the task of national reconstruction.

For this purpose, we have decided to form the National Reconstruction Force (Rashtriya Punarnirman Vahini) which will involve youth from 18 to 35 years of age. This force will focus on basic services in the rural and agricultural sectors, protection of environment, mass movement for population, control, fight against drugs, spread of education, uplift of dalit and tribal women and in the field of sports, art and culture. These youth will also get honorarium for their work. Initially this scheme will be implemented in some districts and finally will be extended all over the country.

This scheme will be launched on January 12, 1999 which is the Birth Anniversary of Swami Vivekanand and which is celebrated as the Youth Day. I call upon the young men and women of this country to donate one year of their youth to rejuvenate the nation.

GOLDEN JUBILEE EDUCATION DEVELOPMENT SCHEME

Satellite Scheme

The next millennium is beckoning us. It will be century of Information Technology. The greatest strength of India is its intellect. India has the third largest trained manpower in the field of Science and Technology. We will have to tap this strength. My Government has taken several new initiatives in the field of Information Technology. It is our ambition that the country should become a super power in this field.

Keeping this in view I am announcing a new initiative. Space is a new race an opportunity to look for innumerable possibilities in the coming century. Space technology has many advantages, which India can utilise to meet the aspirations of its younger generation. On the basis of the slogan Jai Vigyan, my Government wants to fulfil the dreams of our youth. In this direction we will start programmes on a new satellite named Swarna Jayanti Vidya Vikas Antariksh Upagraha Yojana (Golden Jubilee Education Development Space Satellite Scheme).

The first satellite of this programme – INSAT 3-B – will be assembled and launched before August 15, 1999 by the Indian Space Research Organisation (ISRO) within a record time of less than twelve months. Six transponders of this satellite will be available exclusively to execute Operation Knowledge which aims to provide computer, internet and computer based education to all the students of the country. All Universities, engineering and medical colleges, research laboratories and other centres of higher learning particularly will be linked to the Information Technology Network before the next Independence Day. This programme will also fulfil the development related information needs of the states.

ECONOMIC AND SOCIAL INDEPENDENCE

Today 125th birth anniversary celebrations of Maharishi Aurobindo are coming to a close. He visualized the spiritual, moral and cultural renaissance of the country. Today we should pledge to fulfil his dreams.

Bharat Ratna Baba Saheb Ambedkar once said that political freedom is incomplete without economic and social freedom. Today, on our political Independence Day we cannot forget this moot point. In the half-century gone by, we have been able to keep intact our political independence but could not win the battle of economic and social independence. We have not been able to free the country from the clutches of poverty and unemployment. The stigma of illiteracy could not be erased. The monsters of casteism and communalism still are raising their ugly head. Today on India's 51st Independence Day, let us pledge to win economic and social independence.

CAUVERY ACCORD

In the short tenure of my Prime Ministership, I have made an effort to take everybody along and I have practised the politics of consensus. Take the example of Cauvery. There was dispute for years on sharing of Cauvery water among Karnataka, Tamil Nadu, Kerala and Pondicherry. On some occasions, this dispute took a serious turn. Water is used to extinguish fire but if water itself is on fire, what could be done! There is a solution. The solution lies in maturity, harmony, tolerance, patriotism and a willingness to keep others interest in mind. The recently concluded Cauvery Accord epitomises all this.

Is it not surprising that a large amount of water of our rivers flows away into the ocean, while we fight over our share of water? These disputes have been going on for years. This situation has to be changed. Our rivers, which link the states of the country, have to link the hearts of the countrymen too. There is a need to formulate a National Water Policy. We have promised to formulate such a policy. However, it is possible only with everybody's cooperation and patience.

NATIONAL AGENDA FOR GOVERNANCE

My Government has been seriously endeavouring to fulfil the promises made in the National Agenda for Governance. Ours is a coalition and such Governments have their own character which has to be faithfully adhered to. We have prepared a common programme that is the national agenda for our alliance. We have kept all contentious issues out of this arrangement. We have always held national interest to be above the party and personal interest.

The country is passing through a transitional phase today. Our political and administrative system is facing a serious challenge. In such a situation every party and every leader has to conduct himself with a sense of responsibility. History will not forgive us for any action which hurts the nation.

The common man should also ponder over the existing political and administrative set up. We are faced with some basic issues. Are frequent elections ins the interest of the country? Is it the nation's interest to incur heavy expenditures on frequent elections?

NO COMPROMISE ON PRINCIPLES IN PURSUIT OF POWER

I have been Prime Minister only for five months. We have a very thin majority in the Lok Sabha. I am aware of the limitations of the coalition Government. I am also aware that in today's system an innocent sage can be hanged by the power hungry.

I can assure you that I have never compromised on principles in pursuit of power and I will never do it. Being in power or out of power is the same for me. I had been in opposition for years and faithfully performed my duties. My opponents have also commended it. Today, a poem of Dr Shiv Mangal Singh Suman comes to mind:

(I am not afraid of victory or defeat; whatever comes my way on the path of duty, I will accept it as it is and would no task for any favours).

I wish to assure you that till my last breath I will neither ask for favours, nor give up the path of struggle. I only need your support. I only need the blessings of one billion of my countrymen. There comes a moment in life when one stands at crossroads and ponders over the path to take.

(Modesty is being enraged openly and pawn has beaten the queen, should I take one last gambit or leave it all, which path do I take?).

Then I feel that I cannot go into oblivion leaving the challenges behind. I have to struggle. Once again, I reiterate my pledge in your presence from the ramparts of Red Fort.

(I will not accept defeat and will start the struggle afresh. I will write and unwrite my own destiny and sing a new tune.)

Thank you very much. Join me in saying:

Jai Hind

Appendix 4

Tryst with Destiny*

Pt Jawaharlal Nehru

Long years ago we made a tryst with destiny, and now the time comes when we shall redeem our pledge, not wholly or in full measure, but very substantially. At the stroke of the midnight hour, when the world sleeps, India will awake to life and freedom. A moment comes, which comes but rarely in history, when we step out from the old to the new, when an age ends, and when the soul of a nation, long suppressed, finds utterance.

It is fitting that at this solemn moment we take the pledge of dedication to the service of India and her people and to the still larger cause of humanity.

At the dawn of history India started on her unending quest, and trackless centuries which are filled with her striving and the grandeur of her success and her failures. Through good and ill fortune alike she has never lost sight of that quest or

---

* Prime Minister Pt Jawaharlal Nehru's speech on the eve of India's Independence at midnight on 15 August 1947.

forgotten the ideals which gave her strength. We end today a period of ill fortune and India discovers herself again.

The achievement we celebrate today is but a step, an opening of opportunity, to the greater triumphs and achievements that await us. Are we brave enough and wise enough to grasp this opportunity and accept the challenge of the future?

Freedom and power bring responsibility. The responsibility rests upon this assembly, a sovereign body representing the sovereign people of India. Before the birth of freedom we have endured all the pains of labour and our hearts are heavy with the memory of this sorrow. Some of those pains continue even now. Nevertheless, the past is over and it is the future that beckons to us now.

That future is not one of ease or resting but of incessant striving so that we may fulfil the pledges we have so often taken and the one we shall take today. The service of India means the service of the millions who suffer. It means the ending of poverty and ignorance and disease and inequality of opportunity.

The ambition of the greatest man of our generation has been to wipe every tear from every eye. That may be beyond us, but as long as there are tears and suffering, so long our work will not be over.

And so we have to labour and to work, and work hard, to give reality to our dreams. Those dreams are for India, but they are also for the world, for all the nations and peoples are too closely knit together today for anyone of them to imagine that it can live apart.

Peace has been said to be indivisible; so is freedom, so is prosperity now, and so also is disaster in this one world that can no longer be split into isolated fragments.

To the people of India, whose representatives we are, we make an appeal to join us with faith and confidence in this great adventure. This is no time for petty and destructive criticism, no time for ill will or blaming others. We have to build the noble mansion of free India where all her children may dwell.

The appointed day has come – the day appointed by destiny – and India stands forth again, after long slumber and struggle, awake, vital, free and independent. The past clings on to us still in some measure and we have to do much before we redeem the pledges we have so often taken. Yet the turning point is past, and history begins anew for us, the history which we shall live and act and others will write about.

It is a fateful moment for us in India, for all Asia and for the world. A new star rises, the star of freedom in the east, a new hope comes into being, a vision long cherished materialises. May the star never set and that hope never be betrayed!

We rejoice in that freedom, even though clouds surround us, and many of our people are sorrow-stricken and difficult problems encompass us. But freedom brings responsibilities and burdens and we have to face them in the spirit of a free and disciplined people.

On this day our first thoughts go to the architect of this freedom, the father of our nation, who, embodying the old spirit of India, held aloft the torch of freedom and lighted up the darkness that surrounded us.

We have often been unworthy followers of his and have strayed from his message, but not only we but succeeding generations will remember this message and bear the imprint in their hearts of this great son of India, magnificent in his faith and strength and courage and humility. We shall never allow that torch of freedom to be blown out, however high the wind or stormy the tempest.

Our next thoughts must be of the unknown volunteers and soldiers of freedom who, without praise or reward, have served India even unto death.

We think also of our brothers and sisters who have been cut off from us by political boundaries and who unhappily cannot share at present in the freedom that has come. They are of us and will remain of us whatever may happen, and we shall be sharers in their good and ill fortune alike.

The future beckons to us. Whither do we go and what shall be our endeavour? To bring freedom and opportunity to the common man, to the peasants and workers of India; to fight and end poverty and ignorance and disease; to build up a prosperous, democratic and progressive nation, and to create social, economic and political institutions which will ensure justice and fullness of life to every man and woman.

We have hard work ahead. There is no resting for any one of us till we redeem our pledge in full, till we make all the people of India what destiny intended them to be.

We are citizens of a great country, on the verge of bold advance, and we have to live up to that high standard. All of us, to whatever religion we may belong, are equally the children of India with equal rights, privileges and obligations.

We cannot encourage communalism or narrow-mindedness, for no nation can be great whose people are narrow in thought or in action.

To the nations and peoples of the world we send greetings and pledge ourselves to cooperate with them in furthering peace, freedom and democracy.

And to India, our much-loved motherland, the ancient, the eternal and the ever-new, we pay our reverent homage and we bind ourselves afresh to her service.

Jai Hind

Appendix 5

Building a Strong India*

Sardar Vallabhbhai Patel

You want me to talk to you in English. I shall obey your command; but take it from me that it will not be long before you yourselves will have to speak in our national language. If you do not do that, you will drag the country backward. We have to exert our maximum effort to go forward. Unless you do that, I am afraid, you will suffer.

After a prolonged struggle the country has secured the freedom, but it is not the freedom of the kind that we wanted. It is not the freedom of the kind that the deliverer of the country expected, and to our shame we have to confess that by our folly we have lost him. Now after his going we must do penance and try our best to deserve the freedom that he obtained for us.

Free India is only a child of one and a half year. It has yet to learn to walk; it has to grow, to be strong, and its future

* Speech of Deputy Prime Minister Sardar Vallabhbhai Patel at Madras on February 23, 1949.

depends upon how we build today. Therefore, we have to nurse it carefully; we have to feed, clothe and strengthen it properly. It is our great good fortune that we have here a rare opportunity to build our own country in our own fashion. History will record what we are doing today.

The first requisite for building a strong, free India is unity and peace. If there is no unity in the country, it is bound to go down. Therefore we must first of all adjust our differences and behave in such a manner that there is complete harmony and peace in the country. You cannot expect the Government continuously to maintain peace by force. It would be an evil day when in this country the Government has to use repressive measures permanently. Today we are passing through a period of crisis and our young men have, in their impatience, not realised that the freedom which has been obtained with great difficulty is likely to be lost or likely to give no benefit, no advantage, if we do not appreciate that our present duty is to unite and consolidate our freedom.

We lost our leader because we forgot the very first lesson. If we do not realise even after his going that in unity lies our strength, then greater misfortune will befall us.

For unity, we must forget differences of caste and creed and remember that we are all Indians, and all equal. There can be no distinction between man and man in a free country. All must have equal opportunities, equal rights and equal responsibilities. This is difficult to achieve in practice, but we must continuously strive towards that end.

There is one other thing that we have to do to maintain peace and order in this country. For a few years at least, till we are able to stand on our own legs, we must forget that we can every now and then threaten the Government. We cannot function if the Government is to be challenged day after day by groups of people who want to have their own way. What they want may be, according to their own honest thinking, very good; but Gandhiji has put before us the ideal of obtaining what we want by peaceful methods and through truth and non-violence. If people begin to threaten and challenge Government's authority and try to overthrow it to gain their objectives by force, the latter would not be able to do anything constructive. Forces are existing in this country which would create chaos and disorder, which would weaken the country instead of strengthening it.

We in the Government have been dealing with the RSS movement. They want that the Hindu Rajya or Hindu culture should be imposed by force. No government can tolerate this. There are almost as many Muslims in this country as in the part that has been partitioned away. We are not going to drive them away. It would be an evil day if we started that game, in spite of partition and whatever happens. We must understand that they are going to stay here and it is our obligation and our responsibility to make them feel that this is their country. It is, of course, their responsibility, on the other hand, to discharge their duties as citizens of this country.

We must all understand that the partition is behind us. It has to come to stay. I honestly believe that it is good for both the new nations. In two hundred years of a perpetual source of trouble and quarrels, in two hundred years of slavery, the administration created a situation in which we began to drift away from each other. It is good that we have agreed to the partition in spite of all its evils; I have never repented my agreeing to the partition. From the experience of one year of joint administration when we had not agreed to the partition, I know we would have erred grievously and repented if we had not agreed. It would have resulted in a partition not into two countries but into several bits. Therefore, whatever some people may say, I am convinced and I remain convinced that our having agreed to the partition has been for the good of the country.

After the partition, we had a huge problem; those who partitioned the country with our concurrence had mental reservations; they thought that the partition into two is not the last word and they started their game immediately after the partition. They went to Junagadh located in the midst of the Kathiawar states, where nearly half the number of princely states are located. They took Junagadh and secured its accession to Pakistan. It was the first danger sign, the signal for dividing India again. Fortunately for us, we woke up in time and those who tried that game saw that we are not sleeping. Simultaneously, there was trouble in Kashmir. Although there were many difficulties, the Government of India, despite all the impediments, got the situation under control rapidly. I should say we enhanced our reputation by sending there our army, which, in spite of its complete Indianisation, has proved its mettle and proved its worth. It is a great thing that immediately after the partition of the army and the partition of the country, our army, manned absolutely by our own people, showed by their strategy, their valour and their organising ability that it can stand comparison with any army in the world. It is a great gain.

Then our neighbour gave us long sleepless nights. Often, people were angry with us and thought we were neglecting the South. They hardly knew our difficulties and our plans. These plans cannot be revealed. What would happen if Hyderabad was invaded from the outside or if Hyderabad attacked us. We had to make preparations all over India. You know now by the results that we have kept our promise to perform the operation in such a manner that there is the least possible bloodshed. This is what we have to show for the first year of our freedom.

People are impatient; they want more wages for labour. Do they think we want to starve labour? Are we foreigners? Some people say we are capitalist agents. One thing I learnt from Mahatma Gandhi is that a public man should not have any property and I can challenge any Socialist or any Communist to play this game with me. But my quarrel is with those who, contrary to the second part of Mahatmaji's advice to us, want to use violence. There should be no terrorism amongst ourselves. So long as people were playing that game when we were under a foreign power, we made allowance for it; we are paying for it also, because an evil once tolerated grows. That is what we see in Hyderabad.

Why are these Communists creating trouble there? How did they grow? It was because the Hyderabad government was foolish enough to allow them to grow for its own ends and we had no control over them then to be able to suppress them. And what is it that we want there now? In three or four months' time, 200 or more young Congressmen, their own brothers, have been murdered. Is it a sign of the freedom that in the first year of the freedom you got 200 Congressmen killed in cold blood in a small area? Once these terrorists are driven out from that area, where will they go? Inside your border. They will harass you, they will play the same game with you. To the Communists, my appeal may be in vain, because they do not listen. I told them immediately after my release from the jail last time that I was prepared to take all the Communists into the Congress, to forget the past and keep the doors open provided they give up violence and cease to draw their inspiration from the foreign countries. Even now our offer is open, but if terrorism is the only method they want to employ, because they cannot defeat us at the polls and separate us from the masses of India, then it is our misfortune that we have to put our own dear young men and women into prison or to drive them underground.

That is one section of the people with whom we have to deal; the other is the RSS. I have made them an open offer: 'Change your plans, give up secrecy, eschew communal conflict, respect the Constitution of India, show your loyalty to the Flag and make us believe that we can trust your words. To say one thing and to do another is a game which will not do. In one year of the freedom we have experienced many things and learnt many lessons. Whether they are friends or foes, whether they are our own dear young children, we are not going to allow them to play with fire, so that the house is not set on fire. It would be criminal to allow young men to indulge in acts of violence and destruction, to let the lessons that our neighbouring countries have learnt be wasted on us.

Thus I have spoken to the RSS and to the Communists. Then you have our Sikh friends. Some of them have also begun to threaten us and throw challenges. They are the only community in India which is allowed, with the unanimous voice of the Constituent Assembly, to keep arms. No other community is allowed to keep a sword or a *kirpan*. Why did we do this? Not in order that they might threaten the government with the use of force. Government is prepared to hand over power to anybody who can take the people with him. But if anybody is going to play false and threaten the popular government, the latter will not fail the people.

These are some of the many forces we are handling simultaneously in the first or second year of our freedom. We know that we have your affection, your love, your confidence, but that is not enough. You have seen our friends in the Railways threaten us. They say there is going to be a strike in the Railways if we do not meet their demands. We are willing to do so if we can. We would be most anxious to do so. But I must point out to those who are in charge of the Railway union that there are millions in this country who do not get as much as the Railwaymen get; let them not create the forces which they will not be able to control; let the Railwaymen understand that it is also their duty to share the misfortunes of the people in a period of trouble. Let us tide over the difficulty first. After all, the Railway is a nationalised concern; it is not a private company. Imagine the consequences, in this period of trouble, if Railwaymen do not play their part. If there is a strike on the Railways and we have to move the army from one place to another with the Railway communications cut off, one place to another swiftly, as we are faced with the threatened famine. If during such a period the South Indian Railway, which has threatened to strike, goes on strike, who will starve, and what would be the consequences? When the Railway Federation suspended its strike threat and kept it in abeyance, the other group called them capitalist agents. Now these other people have called for a strike; they know that they are in a minority and they will not succeed in making the Railwaymen go on strike. So their only weapon is terrorism, sabotage, dislocation and disorder.

The Provincial Government naturally have to tackle these people and immediately the Federation comes in with a statement that it is a wrong policy. I would like to know what is the right policy. When a house is on fire, is it the right policy to throw petrol or kerosene on it, or water?

We are living in very difficult times; yet the heart of the country is sound. The whole country knows that we are carrying an unbearable burden. Yet if anyone wants to see what the country thinks, let him come to the polls; I am prepared to accept the challenge. I am prepared to vacate as many seats as you like and have a trial of strength. And if you are able to take the country with you, we shall bless you, because the country is not going to follow any path which is foreign to the Indian culture and civilisation and the path that Mahatma Gandhi has shown. But I want to ask you why a few people roundabout the border of Hyderabad are terrorising the people in Krishna district? It is the fault of Congressmen. Are they united? Why are they quarrelling? Why do they not understand their responsibility? We made all kinds of sacrifices all our lives. Why did we make these sacrifices? Let not South India lose its good name and reputation. I appeal to you to realise what is happening. Did you ever imagine that Gandhiji would hear of a Congressman murdering a Congressman, or a Congressman instigating or helping a Communist to murder another

Congressman? If the South Indian Railway is threatened, or if those Railwaymen who work in South India are asked to go on strike, have you no responsibility? Everyone in India has to realise that, as a free citizen of India, he must shoulder graver and greater responsibility if India is to take its proper place amongst the nations of the world.

Yesterday, I was presented an address by the Chambers of Commerce. It was in fact a catalogue of grievances. I had to tell them the unpleasant truth that unless everybody in this country, ie businessmen, labourers, industrialists, students and government, all combine and cooperate, we are not going to make progress . We have not yet put democracy on a sound basis. In a democracy, of course, it is the will of the people that prevails, but the people must have experience to make their own free will felt and must have the responsibility to see that everyone is going to fulfil his obligations.

In this country, the greatest need of the hour is food. We import millions of tons of food into our country. We have not got the ships to bring the food that we want. So we pay crores of rupees as freight charges simply to bring the food here. We have not enough boats even to catch fish. We have no mercantile marine. We have nothing left in this country; for the last 200 years it has been bled white; during the war years in particular, every ounce of blood has been taken out. Our Railway system has been completely disorganised. The Transport Member makes tremendous efforts to set it right. But the Railways are like a decrepit old widow. The Railway sleepers and rails were taken out and sent to various theatres of war. We cannot replace wagons which have been overused for so many years. We cannot get locomotives. We cannot make them here; we have yet to establish factories for meeting the requirements of our country.

We must have a good mercantile marine; so we are building a fine port at Vizagapatnam. But it is only a beginning. A small country like Portugal has got pockets on our soil; we also have French colonies. Our friends in these areas who are fighting for the freedom along with us ask us to first settle this question; others talk of the wages for labour; and still others want us to deal with the businessmen first and to give them their due. The businessmen are frightened of the talk of nationalisation. They Say: "unless you give us condition in which Industry can thrive, we cannot invest money or we cannot get money." So production has been at a standstill. We cannot produce more wealth in this country. The Communists and the Socialists say: "let us first divide whatever is left and be all poor." But if you do not produce anything, then neither you nor any other section of the people will have anything. Therefore, so far as food is concerned, I have a grievance against the Congressmen and against those people who are in the Congress and today are preaching to peasants not to help this Government in procurement and to ask for more money. They are not better than the other people who say: "Do not work, stop work, go slow, ask for more wages." Because if there is no procurement, then the only course open to us is to import more and more, and importing more is nothing but economic ruin of this country.

If we in this country realise our responsibility, there will be no dearth of food. Of course, there is scarcity to a certain extent; the shortage of food according to our statistics is 7 per cent; in a vast country like this, if we act up to our responsibilities, this is negligible. Many people waste their food and cook more than they should. Those people should put a stop to this wastage. Then we should produce more food. Every inch of land that is available should be used for growing vegetables, fruit and other food. Wherever there is waste land which can be reclaimed, it would be the duty of the Government, local bodies, zamindars, and every citizen of India to use all his resources in the immediate task of growing more food on it. Thirdly, whatever surplus you have got, give it to the Government. When your neighbours are starving, do not be selfish. That is not the way which Gandhiji showed us. That is not our culture. Let not our neighbour starve; we must share his misery. Educate the peasants; tell them it is a religious duty to give all of their surplus for Government procurement, so that the Government can decrease the imports.

There are many Congressmen who are indifferent to this matter. They think that the elections are coming and they will be unpopular if they ask for procurement. A greater crime is committed by those who teach the peasants to ask for higher prices and not to give crops for procurement. That is a crime against humanity. A real Congressman would say: "My friends, our neighbours are dying; our country is being ruined; let us share the suffering of our brothers." I am saying harsh things to the Congressmen because they have a greater responsibility, greater influence and a greater hold on the people.

Let us all put our heads as well as our hands together, tighten up our belts and be prepared to share the sufferings for a while. It is only for a while, because I assure you that the economy of the country is sound; the heart of the country is sound; there is immense wealth in the country. The country is full of mineral resources and wealth. We have simply to use our brains and our resources to take them out and use them. But it will take time; it is not an easy thing. We shall require experts, machinery and capital goods. If we tide over this short period, India will be flowing with milk and honey.

Index